Logan The Mingo
A Story Of The Frontier

H. R. Gordon

Alpha Editions

This Edition Published in 2021

ISBN: 9789354366697

Design and Setting By
Alpha Editions
www.alphaedis.com
Email – info@alphaedis.com

As per information held with us this book is in Public Domain.
This book is a reproduction of an important historical work. Alpha Editions uses the best technology to reproduce historical work in the same manner it was first published to preserve its original nature. Any marks or number seen are left intentionally to preserve its true form.

CONTENTS

CHAPTER	PAGE
I. A FOREST MESSENGER	1
II. ANOTHER FOREST MESSENGER	10
III. A BIG BLACK BEAR	19
IV. A TEACHER AND A PUPIL	26
V. A MASTER AND TWO PUPILS	35
VI. THREE OLD FRIENDS	43
VII. LAME PANTHER AND LOGAN	51
VIII. A DEFIANCE	61
IX. "GOOD-NIGHT, MY BROTHER"	70
X. A FEW LIVELY MINUTES	78
XI. AUNT CYNTHIA'S ASTONISHED CALLER	87
XII. WITHIN THE CABIN	94
XIII. THE COUNCIL OF WAR	103
XIV. AN UNEXPECTED PRESENT	111
XV. SPEAKING WITH A DOUBLE TONGUE	118
XVI. THE MINGO'S RETURN	127
XVII. AS UNDER A FLAG OF TRUCE	135
XVIII. A STARTLING VISITOR	143
XIX. OOROMOO	151
XX. AT THE THREE ROCKS	159
XXI. A STRANGE INTERVIEW	168
XXII. THE SIGNAL FIRE	177

Contents

CHAPTER	PAGE
XXIII. A SLIP	186
XXIV. OUT INTO THE NIGHT	196
XXV. HOW THE WARNING REACHED FORT DINWIDDIE	203
XXVI. ALL READY AND WAITING	212
XXVII. DIAMOND CUT DIAMOND	221
XXVIII. A VAIN HUNT	228
XXIX. AN INSIDIOUS ADVERSARY	238
XXX. CHIEFTAIN AND CAPTAIN	245
XXXI. TRENDING TO THE NORTHWARD	255
XXXII. AN EARLY CAMP	264
XXXIII. HIDE AND SEEK WITH DANGER	273
XXXIV. STRANGE DOINGS	289
XXXV. KNIGHT AND LADY	300
XXXVI. AUNT CYNTHIA IS ENCOURAGED IN THE GOOD WAY	313
XXXVII. HOW SEVERAL THINGS HAPPENED	323
XXXVIII. CONCLUSION	331

LOGAN THE MINGO

A STORY OF THE FRONTIER

CHAPTER I

A FOREST MESSENGER

ON a crisp autumn day, many years ago, Arthur Oakland, a lusty Virginian youth in his teens, left his cabin home to the westward of the Alleghany Mountains, to attend to the most serious business of his life.

He was a fine type of the frontier young men, who, trained from early childhood in toil, hardship, endurance, danger, and woodcraft, struck brave blows for the mother country in the French and Indian War, that supreme struggle between England and France for the mastery of the American continent, and later for the independence of their native land, through the trying years from Lexington to Yorktown. He was tall, muscular, and active, with clear blue eyes, ruddy cheeks, soft brown hair, and an alertness of manner that told of his training in the woods, and the high spirits and rugged health which fitted him to hold his own among the veterans of the settlements.

He was clothed in homespun, the product of the spinning-wheel deftly handled by his industrious mother. His shoes were heavy and serviceable, and his cap of coonskin served him equally well during the flaming heat of midsummer or when the wintry sleet and snow stung his face like needle-points. A child of half his years would have scorned as unseemly luxuries much which in these modern days we look upon as necessities.

Armed with flintlock rifle, powder-horn, bullet-pouch, and hunting-knife, Arthur Oakland bade his parents good-bye on that autumn morning, and walked with strong rapid stride along a faintly marked trail which led toward a small tributary of one of the main streams that wound its way along the westward slope of the mountain range. The ground rose rapidly, and he pressed forward until he had come to a more elevated portion. The task would have made you and me puff and gasp, but when he paused close to an immense, jagged, spreading rock, his respiration was as deliberate as when he passed out of the door of his own humble home. Leaning his rifle against the mass of stone, he set himself to work gathering dead twigs, limbs, and leaves, which were carefully piled on top of the rock, until a considerable heap was collected. The ashes and remnants which had not been blown away showed that this was not the first time a similar flame had been kindled there. Then with his flint and tinder the lad set fire to the crisp, dry leaves which quickly communicated with the twigs until the whole mass was speedily burning right merrily. The air was so still that the heavy smoke rose almost perpendicularly into the clear sky and was visible for miles in every direction.

Arthur picked up his rifle and stepping back several paces among the bowlders and stunted pines watched the progress of the small fire. He was so expert at this sort of work that he knew from the first it would be no failure. His manner clearly showed that the smoke was intended as a signal to some one.

"It 'll do," he said to himself, as he turned away from the crackling blaze and pushed on with the same resolute step to the westward. "Stanton will see that and will know I am coming. But," added the youth, "he does n't dream of the message I am taking to him and Aunt Cynthia this time, and there is n't a minute either for me to lose."

The young man whom I have introduced to you was the only child of James and Mary Oakland, who dwelt in the little frontier settlement of Warrenburg, which was protected by a strong blockhouse and lay some twenty miles to the eastward of the home of Winslow Bothwell, a widower, who lived with his maiden sister Cynthia and his son Stanton, of about the same age as Arthur Oakland. Being such close neighbors, it was natural that the two boys should become the most intimate of chums and that they should frequently visit back and forth. It was the custom of either when about to set out on such a visit to announce it by means of a signal fire such as has just been described. This insured the other being "at home," whereas but for such notice he might go off on some hunt that would keep him for hours and perhaps days in the woods.

Such being the fact, you would not suppose there was anything calling for special mention in the display of the signal fire by Arthur Oakland on this sunshiny afternoon in autumn, since the same thing had been done many times. But herein lay the great difference and the alarming significance of the action: the time was the eve of the breaking out of the French and Indian War, mutterings of which had been heard so long that many had settled into the belief that it would never come at all. But the elder Bothwell and Mr. Oakland were not among these, and it was agreed between them that as soon as the latter learned of any impending peril, he should notify the other at once. That time had arrived, for the scouts attached to the blockhouse, a number of whom were continually wandering through the surrounding wilderness, brought in startling news of the hostile movements of the Indians and French, the latter inciting the former to activity. The only hope for the Bothwell family was to leave their home immediately and make all haste to the protection of Warrenburg and its blockhouse.

So you will understand the anxiety of young Arthur Oakland when he set out from his home to warn his friends of their peril. He and Stanton were cousins, since their mothers were sisters, and the tie of comradeship between them could not have been stronger.

Naturally when Arthur had set his signal fire going, he peered searchingly to the westward in quest of an answer. The boys often exchanged such messages, though not always, and the youth thought nothing of it when the minutes passed without bringing him a reply. As he descended the slope, he caught many glimpses of the country and sky to the westward, so that an answer to his signal could not have escaped his eye. When fifteen or twenty minutes had passed, however, he saw something which he did not wish to see; for to the northwest a thin, wavy column of vapor climbed aloft and was sharply outlined against the blue sky beyond. He stopped short and studied it with misgiving.

"That is n't Stant," he exclaimed, "for it is in the wrong direction and it is n't the kind of signal he uses."

The smoke instead of ascending in a clear, even column, was broken and wavy, showing that it was manipulated by the one who had started it. Such signals are sometimes seen at the present day in the Southwest, when an Apache or Arapahoe smothers the smoke at regular intervals with his blanket. By that method those red men telegraph messages from mountain-top to mountain-top over hundreds of miles of territory.

"That means Indians," was the conclusion of the youth; "but what they are driving at is more than I can tell. I wonder whether it has anything to do with *my* signal."

He scanned the sky in all directions, but could discover nothing that looked like a reply, nor could he figure out the meaning of the display, except that it indicated danger. The one comfort was that it was not between him and the home of his cousin, for had it been, he might well doubt his ability to help his friends; for they would be shut off from reaching the settlement, except by a roundabout journey, in which the chances would be overwhelmingly against their escape.

Now it must be stated at this point that the means by which Arthur Oakland made his way to the home of his cousin was what might be termed a mixed one, since it was generally by land and water. At a comparatively short distance from Warrenburg, it was his custom to enter his canoe, which he propelled up the tributary already referred to until it grew so narrow, broken, and swift that the small craft could be driven no farther. Then it was run upon the shelving wooded bank, and the remaining five or six miles were made over a clearly marked trail, which led up the mountainous slope to the broad, natural, and cultivated clearing where his uncle and aunt had made their home for a number of years.

On this morning the youth was about to set out in his canoe, when he was arrested by a strange, wild, resounding cry that vibrated among the forest arches, coming seemingly from a point nearly a mile to the northwest, and therefore in the direction of the Indian signal fire. He stopped and listened thinking it would be repeated, as was the case, for within two or three minutes it rang out again, and though it seemed to issue from the same point, yet the trained ear of the young hunter told him it was nearer than before.

"That sounds like Aunt Cynthia," he said thoughtfully, "for she has such a sharp voice that she can make it reach miles in any direction."

The minutes passed, but the cry was not repeated,

and then Arthur made a sort of funnel with one of his hands and sent out a clear, penetrating response, which might have served as the echo of the first call that had fallen upon his ears. That it was heard by the other was proven when once more the cry reverberated among the rocks and trees. At the same time he began cautiously picking his way over and through the rough country which intervened between him and the stranger.

For a time the youth uttered no sound, but his senses were on the alert, and he used his eyes and ears to the highest point of which they were capable, and you need not be reminded that in that respect none could have excelled him. Since the two were drawing near each other, although at a moderate pace, the intervening distance steadily lessened. Arthur was listening for another call, when it suddenly came from a point that was not half as far away as when first heard.

This time he abruptly paused, for there was a tone in the sound that he had not noticed at first, though he was never fully free from misgiving. While he could not have mistaken the cry for that of any person except his relative, yet there was something in its peculiar *timbre*, so to speak, which suggested her voice, while the suspicion that it came from her was strengthened by the singular situation already described.

A grim smile lit up the handsome face of the youth, who ceased picking his way through the solitude and stood still, within a couple of paces of a twisted, gnarled oak, whose trunk was fully three feet in diameter. Listening and peering intently about him, he was as motionless as the tree itself. When fully ten minutes had passed without bringing a repetition of the response, he deliberately emitted the call, and then fixed his eyes upon the point from which he expected the answer to come.

And come it did,—round, full, and clear, and from a spot that at the most could not have been more than a hundred yards distant. Without a moment's hesitation, Arthur repeated the call and then did a singular thing. He stepped behind the gnarled oak and deliberately raised the hammer of his rifle.

CHAPTER II

ANOTHER FOREST MESSENGER

ARTHUR OAKLAND knew the exact point where the stranger must appear. It was from among a clump of pines, not fifty yards off, and between which and himself was a stretch of natural opening.

The dull click of the hammer of his rifle had hardly sounded when he raised the weapon to a level with his shoulder and carefully sighted it alongside the trunk of the oak behind which he had sheltered himself. For, instead of a woman or man who came into sight, it was an animal, lithe, sinewy, brown in color, and with the springy lightness of a cat, to which species it belonged, being an American panther, known in more southern countries as the catamount or cougar, and generally called on the frontier a "painter." It is one of the fiercest and most dangerous creatures found in our forests, and of course was far more plentiful a hundred years ago than to-day.

At the moment the brute thrust its head into sight, following with its graceful body and making no more noise than a shadow, it emitted the peculiar cry which many a time has been mistaken for that of a human being. Arthur instantly replied, all the time holding his gun on a dead level and sighting along the barrel at his foe. It turned like a flash and looked at the point whence came the answer to its call. It saw the coonskin cap and side of the face at the stock of the rifle, and its jaws were parted as, with a low, cavernous growl, it took a stealthy step forward, but before it could follow with a second, the youth pressed the trigger of his gun.

The aim was perfect, and the bullet, entering the body just below the neck and above the forelegs, bored its way through the heart of the panther, who, with an ear-splitting screech, leaped high in air, dropped on its side, and rolling over and over and furiously clawing the dirt, quickly became motionless.

"Well, my friend," remarked Arthur, proceeding to reload his weapon, "you set out to fool me, but it looks as if *you* were the one who was fooled."

Having disposed of the brute in this summary fashion, the youth gave it no further thought. He did not even go forward to make a closer inspection, but, walking to the little stream mentioned, pushed his canoe into the water, laid his gun across the gunwales in front, and swinging the paddle with the skill of a Nippinock warrior, sent it skimming like a swallow against the current.

While thus engaged, he saw that his course was taking him toward the camp-fire which had first caught his attention and caused him so much misgiving. Recalling the wavy appearance of the telltale smoke, he noticed that the peculiarity no longer showed. He remembered having heard the scouts and rangers at the fort tell of manipulating the vapor from their camp-fires in that manner, so that the practice was not confined to the red men alone, and might have been resorted to by a party of whites experimenting or practising. Be that as it may, Arthur determined to learn what it all meant, for, as will be noted, the identity of the party was likely to have much to do with the welfare of his own friends. It was not impossible that they were Frenchmen, for the emissaries of the King of France were continually passing through the western country and stirring up the different tribes to hostility against the Americans and English.

With his powerful, tireless sweep, the youth drove his canoe forward until the best point for landing had been reached. Forcing the prow fully a yard up the bank, he sprang ashore and drew the craft still farther out of the water, where there was no danger of its being swept away by a sudden rise of the stream. Then he strode into the wood, and passing around rocks, bowlders, and through undergrowth, briars, and among trees, all the time going straight and true, and watchful against running into any Indian trap, he speedily came upon an interesting scene.

A party of eight or nine men and a dozen horses, several of which were pack animals, had halted beside a brook of crystalline water, fringed with grass so rich and succulent, despite the lateness of the season, that it afforded good nourishment for the horses, which had been relieved of saddles, bridles, and their burdens, and were vigorously cropping the herbage.

A big fire had been kindled, over which slices of venison, procured earlier in the day, had been broiled, with the skill of veteran frontiersmen. Indeed, the dinner had already been eaten, and the company would soon resume their long wilderness journey toward the northwest.

Arthur was surprised that no pickets were stationed, but the alertness of the men was shown by their discovery of him before he gained a fair sight of them. One glance was sufficient to inform the travellers he was a friend, and he was allowed to approach unchallenged.

Nearly all of the party had assumed easy lolling postures, like those wearied from long riding in the saddle, and most of them were smoking pipes.

Seated on a fallen tree, a few feet from the fire, were two men who instantly caught the attention of the youth, especially as one of them was an old acquaintance, who had often visited Fort Dinwiddie and had sat at the table of James Oakland. He was also smoking, and his long formidable rifle leaned at his side against the log upon which he sat. He was attired in the usual border costume, resembling that of Arthur himself, except that he wore large boots reaching above his knees into which his buckskin trousers were tucked.

His face was seamed with wrinkles and as brown as an Indian's, made so by years of exposure to storm, heat, sunshine, and wintry cold. He was in middle life, with muscles of iron and the quickness and courage of a panther. His black hair showed only a few streaks of silver, and his bright gray eyes were as penetrating as an eagle's. His name was Christopher Gist, and he was the most famous scout in the employ of the Ohio Land Company.

Seated upon a large stone in front of Gist and talking with him was a much younger person, whom Arthur Oakland viewed with admiration, for physically he was the finest man upon whom he had ever looked. He was more than six feet in height, with large hands and feet, massive shoulders and chest, and the evident strength of a Hercules. His face was smooth, his complexion florid, his eyes of a mild blue, and his hair inclined to be sandy. While he could not be called specially handsome, the expression of his face was kindly and winning. His dress was half military, and, like Gist, he wore high-topped boots into which his buckskin breeches were thrust.

As he talked, he occasionally smiled, displaying a fine set of white, even teeth, unstained by tobacco, but not once did he laugh outright. His rifle reposed against the large stone which served him as a seat, and he held a twig in one hand, whose elbow was supported on an up-gathered knee, while he nibbled at the end of the tiny branch, biting off and spitting away bits as one often does unconsciously, and flicking the twig about his shapely leg when not engaged in wrenching off the other end with his strong teeth.

Gist suddenly took the pipe from between his lips and looked at the boy who was walking toward him, with assurance and yet with becoming modesty.

"Well, if here is n't my old friend Arthur Oakland!" exclaimed the scout, extending his free right hand, his left holding his pipe, while he did not rise from the log.

"How do you do, Mr. Gist?" said the youth, taking the offered hand and returning the cordial pressure.

"I 'm not as feeble as I was, Arthur; set down aside me and tell me how 's your good father and mother."

"They never were better, thank you."

"Serves 'em right! Ah, Major, this is my friend, Arthur Oakland."

The lad rose to his feet and bowed with a feeling of awe when the massive, superb officer arose, took his hand, and gravely said:

"Arthur, I am pleased to make your acquaintance; you seem to be quite a distance from home."

"I have been a good deal farther, sir," replied the lad with a smile as the two resumed their seats; "but my father tells me matters are looking ill."

"He tells you truly," was the reply of the young officer, as gravely as he had spoken before; "the outlook is gloomy, for the French show little disposition to do that which is manifestly right."

"All we can do, Major," said Gist cheerily, as he resumed his pipe, "is to teach 'em better manners; I know *you'll* not be backward in your part when the time comes."

The face of the officer flushed slightly as he modestly replied:

"We will all strive to do our duty, Mr. Gist."

"We have started on a long journey," said the guide to Arthur; "we left Williamsburg several days ago and are heading for the northwest corner

WASHINGTON, GIST, AND ARTHUR OAKLAND.

Another Forest Messenger

of Pennsylvania. The Major there bears a letter from Governor Dinwiddie to the French commander in that part of the world. The Governor did n't read the letter to us," added Gist, with a grin that doubled the number of wrinkles on his seamed countenance, "but it aint much trouble to guess what it says."

"I suppose it is a notice to the French to leave our territory?"

"There aint no doubt of it."

"Do you think they will go?" asked Arthur, deeply interested.

"Yes—when we drive 'em out, and not afore. Them folks like fighting as well as us and they know how to put up a good row."

"There is no mistake as to that," said the officer, compressing his lips and inclining his head.

"But the Virginians and English can fight better."

"Yes; I think so."

"It is a long journey that you have before you," remarked Arthur Oakland.

"One thousand miles, there and back, and it is now so late in autumn that it 'll be the dead of winter afore we see Williamsburg again."

"And it is a wild, unknown country through which you have to pass."

"Every bit of it; we 've got to cross mountains, swim and wade streams, travel hundreds of miles without seeing a living person, but liable in many places to run into a hornets' nest in the shape of a gang of redskins, who 'll risk their own scalps to git ours, while if we meet a lot of bloody Frenchmen, there 'll be music in the air."

The officer looked as if ill-pleased with these plain words.

"Why speak thus, Mr. Gist, when no good can come from it?"

"Nor any harm."

"But you magnify our work, which is another form of boasting."

"Begging your pardon, I 'll drop it."

Arthur remained only a brief while longer, for he saw preparations on the part of the company to resume their journey. He courteously saluted his two friends and withdrew. Gist walked a few paces with him.

"Mr. Gist," said the youth, "who is that officer you called 'Major'?"

"He is a young Virginian, only twenty-two years old. His name is George Washington, and I like him; I think, if he gets a fair show, he 'll amount to something."

History seems to have justified the belief of Christopher Gist, the famous guide.

CHAPTER III

A BIG BLACK BEAR

THE bright keen afternoon was drawing to a close when Arthur Oakland turned his back on the party whose journey through the wilderness has won a place in American history. All my readers have learned the particulars of that exploit of the sturdy young Virginian, George Washington, who, after travelling five hundred miles through the wild region, found the French officer he sought, delivered his letter, and brought back his reply to Governor Dinwiddie, the return journey being made mostly in the depth of winter, and accompanied by hardships and perils such as few men could have overcome. And the reply brought by Washington was the cause of the French and Indian War.

What Arthur had seen and heard confirmed the tidings which he was carrying to his uncle. While the danger of his exposed situation may not have been immediate, yet it was unwise for him to delay his departure. The expectation was that Bothwell, his sister, and son would make their removal on the morrow, and it was the wish of James Oakland that his boy should remain over night and assist in the work. Mr. Bothwell was the owner of a cow, and some simple furniture, a portion of which he would wish to carry away with him. The care of the animal would compel him to make the entire journey by land, no difficult task under the circumstances, since such a journey had been made often enough to imprint a faintly marked path throughout the entire distance between his home and the town of Warrenburg.

The point where Arthur had landed was within less than a mile of that at which he was accustomed to leave his canoe and make the rest of the journey on foot. He found his boat undisturbed, and shoving off, resumed his paddling with the same even, lusty vigor as at first.

The boys generally gave themselves a day in which to complete the journey in either direction, though it was much the easier in going to the eastward, since the canoe had the strong current in its favor. But there being no haste in the matter, the boys did not make a very early start and looked upon the absence of food as nothing. Had they craved it their own skill and the abundance of game would have made the task of obtaining it slight, but the certainty of a good, well served meal awaiting them at their destination was an inducement for postponement that had its effect.

The region was wild and to the untrained woodman forbidding. The current had already become so powerful that Arthur's progress was lessened, and it was apparent that the return passage over this portion of the stream was but play. There were eddies around rocks, some of which were below and some above the surface, and which warned the youth to be on the alert. The shores were rocky, some of the masses of stone being of immense size and rising to a height of thirty or forty feet. Between, around, and among them grew trees and vegetation, most of the former being pines, which are plentiful in that section of the country. Other species of wood were found in the forest, but the leaves dropped from most of them in every swaying breeze, and the wind's moaning among the naked branches was dismal and in darkness sounded like the sighing of the spirits of the air.

But a strong, active lad with rugged health thinks nothing of such things when on his way to visit a playmate. About all that occurred to Arthur Oakland was that his turning aside to call upon Christopher Gist and Major George Washington had so delayed him that he could not expect to reach the home of his cousin before the close of the afternoon.

"And if I make any more such halts it will be night," he reflected.

More in obedience to his training than through

fear of any danger, he continued his searching glances at every point that came under observation. He had not gone far when he discovered something that would have eluded your eyes and mine.

"I wonder what he 's up to," muttered the youth, so slackening his efforts that he barely held the canoe head on to the strong current.

It was on a wooded bluff, less than a hundred yards distant and on the right bank of the stream, that the object which interested him appeared. The bluff was twenty feet in height, and the pines grew almost to its edge. Among these appeared the front of a wild animal, which, although mostly concealed by the vegetation, was revealed to that extent that he recognized it as a large black bear. Moreover, it was evident the brute had been quick to observe the youth and was scrutinizing him.

The situation was peculiar, but there was nothing in it to cause the lad any alarm. It would be absurd to suppose that a sturdy youth of sixteen years, with a loaded rifle within instant reach, would do anything except welcome a meeting with the most formidable animal found in the forests of that region.

Arthur studied the vaguely disclosed beast and was able to make out clearly the head and shoulders, but the rest of the bulky body was hidden among the trees and undergrowth.

"There's enough for me," he concluded, laying down his paddle and catching up his rifle; "I'll cure him of his impudence in watching me without permission."

But the boy forgot one thing for the moment. The current was so swift that before he could sight his weapon the canoe began drifting with it, and not only that, but it spun part way around, so disconcerting him that he dropped his gun and again caught up the long paddle.

The new danger was more imminent than he supposed, for the paddle, instead of sinking deep in the water, as he expected, slid over the face of a rock that was only two or three inches below the surface. He attempted to jam the end against the side, but, before he could do so, the frail structure overturned like a flash.

But Arthur Oakland was equal to the occasion. Seeing that the canoe was going, he leaped lightly out, landing upon the rock, where the water would not have covered his ankles but for its rippling against them. With inimitable dexterity he held the boat with one foot thrust over it, and caught the rifle in his left while he retained the paddle in his right hand. It was an awkward position and he was greatly handicapped, but, remarkable as it may seem, he righted the canoe, first freeing it of all but an insignificant amount of water, and then, making sure it was in a deeper part of the current, he stepped lightly within and immediately assumed mastery of the treacherous craft.

"It was *your* fault," he exclaimed impatiently, alluding to the bear, "and I'll pay you for it!"

Giving his whole attention for some minutes to the boat, he waited until he had secured a position where it was safe to let it drift for a short time, when he again dropped the paddle and caught up his gun. In an instant he had levelled it at the top of the bluff, when lo! there was no bear in sight.

"I suppose he was disgusted with my performance but he sha'n't get away from me in that style."

He drove his boat against the bank, leaped out, and drew the canoe after him. The distance to the bluff was so short and the time that had passed so brief that he was confident of gaining the coveted shot at the bear. Instead of going directly to the spot, he followed a circuitous course that took him deeper into the wood and allowed him to approach the bluff by a route that he hoped would meet the brute.

Arthur moved noiselessly and with great care, for though the bear is naturally a stupid animal, some of them have been known to show a remarkable degree of cunning, and it is a curious fact that while the colossal grizzly of the Far West has little wit, the cinnamon species resembles the fox in its intelligence and "cuteness."

The lad saw nothing of his intended victim, and drew near enough to the bluff to make sure it was not there. Then, as nothing more remained to be done, he started to return to his canoe.

In doing so he kept close to the stream, since that was the shortest course; but he had not taken twenty steps when he made an extraordinary discovery. He was obliged to cross a small depressed place, where the ground was so damp and soft that the footprints of the lightest animal would show.

The bear had taken the same route, and there were the plainly marked impressions of his feet, traceable for a distance of several yards.

But as Arthur Oakland looked his heart gave a great throb, for the prints were not those of a bear, but unmistakably those of moccasins!

"That bear was n't a bear, but an Indian!" he whispered to himself, looking furtively around, "and he is n't far off!"

CHAPTER IV

A TEACHER AND A PUPIL

IT was an alarming discovery, the full meaning of which flashed upon Arthur Oakland. The Indian, when he appeared on top of the bluff, was too cunning to show more of himself than the head and shoulders, since any further display would have revealed his disguise to the keen eyes of the youth. Having effectually deceived him, the warrior quietly withdrew.

It was a terrifying situation, for at the very opening of the singular meeting the lad was taken at a fatal disadvantage. A score of questions flashed through his mind, all of which were difficult, if not impossible, to answer. Why had the Indian shown himself at all? Manifestly, nothing was easier than for him to remain unseen, and, taking deliberate aim from cover, pick off the youth before he dreamed of danger. In truth, he might have done the same, not only before detection, but afterward.

The only theory that presented itself to Arthur was that his enemy, feeling absolutely sure of his victim, was disposed to play with him as a cat does with a mouse.

The lad had halted midway between the bluff and the point where he pulled the canoe up the bank, and grasping his rifle with both hands, peered cautiously around in quest of his foe, debating with himself what was best to do.

Off to the left, as he stood, the wood was quite dense, and he was among a number of goodly sized trees, capable of affording him fair protection. A feeling that whatever peril threatened was from the forest in that direction, with its rocks, bowlders, and undergrowth, caused him to scrutinize that portion of his field of vision with the greatest closeness.

Something flickered, like the passing of a shadow, and almost at the same moment the twilight was lit up by a flash, there was a sharp report, and he distinctly felt the bullet whizz past his cheek, as it skimmed across the stream behind him; and then it was that Arthur Oakland did a thing that displayed a woodcraft which was wonderful in one of his years.

You need not be reminded that percussion or repeating firearms were unknown during the period we have in mind. The flintlock was universally used with musket and the clumsy pistols, and when one of the former weapons was discharged the most expert hunter needed considerable time, the circumstances being considered, in which to reload. The charge was poured from the unstopped powder-horn into the palm of the hand and then allowed to stream down the inclined barrel; the wadding was hammered on top with the ramrod, the spherical bullet pressed gently but firmly upon that, powder poured into the pan, and the hammer, clasping the flint, drawn back before the weapon was ready for use.

All this was well known to Arthur Oakland, who knew also that he could dash across the space separating him from his enemy before the latter had time to reload. The charge was in the gun of the youth, and had the Indian been visible he would have returned the shot on the instant; but the savage had fired from cover, seemingly behind the trunk of a large oak. Arthur could not mistake the spot, and with scarcely a second's hesitation, he broke into a run, leaping over the smaller bowlders, dashing around the larger ones and the trunks of the trees, and crashing through the undergrowth, with his gaze fixed upon the place and his rifle held ready to raise and fire the instant he caught sight of the redskin.

His heart beat fast, for he felt that the crisis was at hand. A few moments more and the dusky miscreant would be at his mercy.

Slackening his pace, as he drew near the oak, he shifted his gun so that it was held at his side, the muzzle pointing forward, the left hand grasping the barrel near the middle, while the right closed around the hammer, with the forefinger resting on the trigger. In this position he could shoot unerringly across the slight space without raising the stock to his shoulder.

"I suppose he is reloading as fast as he knows how," was the thought of Arthur, "but he can't save himself. He came pretty near hitting me, but the miss means his death."

But lo again! Carefully skirting the tree, Arthur Oakland awoke to the amazing fact that the Indian was gone! With lightning stealth he had dodged to other cover upon seeing the failure of his shot.

"That beats all!" exclaimed the disgusted youth; "he has tricked me again!"

He glanced here and there, but saw nothing of the redskin. His straining sense of hearing caught a faint clicking sound, but it was so indistinct that he could not tell from what point of the compass it came.

There was, however, no mistaking its meaning. It was the noise made by the Indian reloading his rifle, and the miscreant was crouching somewhere within stone's throw of the youth, who saw him not nor could he guess where he was. A few more seconds and he would be ready for another shot, which could not fail of its aim.

One thing was clear: it would not do for the lad to stand a moment longer in the open. The faint noise was scarcely heard when with one bound he placed himself behind the trunk of the very oak that had screened the Indian.

But the fearful fact confronted him that he could not know whether as he stood thus he was not in as plain view of his enemy as when in the open, for, though all his senses were keyed to the highest tension, it was out of his power to locate the spot whence came the faint sound whose meaning could not be mistaken.

Like an animal at bay, beset on all sides, Arthur glanced here, there, and everywhere, ready to dart to the other side of the trunk the instant he learned whence the deadly peril threatened.

He reflected that his enemy must aim his weapon at him before firing, and he hoped he would detect it in time to make a quick shift of position. The chances of doing this, however, were so overwhelmingly remote that his real reliance was on his sense of hearing. The old-fashioned flintlock gave out two dull clicks when the hammer was drawn back, and in the profound stillness the youth was certain of hearing them.

And so he did. They pierced the air with startling distinctness, and with a shiver of dread he identified the point whence they came as directly behind him. He was in as plain sight of the Indian as was the trunk of the oak itself!

Did he whisk around to the other side of the shaggy column of bark? No feat of legerdemain was ever performed with more surprising quickness.

"Now, confound you!" grimly muttered the youth, "get the better of me if you can!"

And the Indian straightway proceeded to do it!

In truth, Arthur Oakland was the pupil and his enemy the master in this remarkable test of woodcraft.

The lad, having definitely fixed in his mind the spot where the Indian had finished reloading his rifle and was awaiting another chance to fire, saw that in this remarkable encounter it was the first shot that would decide the issue.

In the second instance the Indian had not used a tree for a refuge, but dropped behind a bowlder, barely two feet in height and less than three times as wide. It was impossible for him to fire from the rear and over this stone without exposing his head and shoulders, and Arthur was confident he could anticipate him.

But the situation was peculiar, though it has been repeated hundreds of times since, as it was hundreds of times before, on the frontier. Every reader of these pages is familiar with the story of the white hunter who, from his concealment behind one tree, drew the fire of the Indian screened by another, by cautiously thrusting his cap, resting on the muzzle of his gun, into sight. Then, when the redskin with a "wild whoop" leaped into view and rushed forward to scalp his victim, that victim calmly raised his gun and despatched the warrior to his happy hunting grounds.

Now, I do not believe any such occurrence ever took place, for no Indian, trained from infancy in the devious trickeries of woodcraft, could be deceived by so simple an artifice. Neither Arthur Oakland nor the warrior a few rods away resorted to it; for had the thought of the plan come to either, he could not have failed to see its uselessness.

However, there must be an end of some nature to the strained situation, for no two enemies can harm each other so long as they are mutually beyond reach. Arthur was disturbed by the thought that night was at hand. In the impenetrable gloom of the wood, the Indian would have the mastery and the boy knew it. The curious encounter must be decided soon, or, if undecided, the youth had to find some way of withdrawing from the spot and placing himself beyond reach of the redskin.

The temptation to glance from behind the tree was irresistible; but, instead of gradually shoving his head to one side, Arthur made a quick flirt, the movement being so rapid that the most alert enemy had no time in which to aim and fire.

The lad saw nothing, which might well be, since it was to be presumed that the Indian was waiting for him to expose himself.

"He's too smart to be fooled and I'm too smart for him——"

Again the report of a rifle rang through the forest arches, and for a moment Arthur Oakland believed he had been fatally hit. He was stunned and blinded by the tiny fragments of bark that were showered into his face, but although the bullet which did this had passed as near as the former, he was not struck.

His first thought was that a second Indian had appeared on the scene, and, while it was remarkable that he too missed his target, yet, if two enemies confronted him, the situation of the youth was hopeless, since the trunk of no tree, even as large as the giants of the Yosemite, can effectually interpose against more than one foe, holding widely separated positions; but brief reflection convinced Arthur that he was confronted by the same Indian, who, by his marvellous woodcraft, had made an important change of his own position without giving any knowledge of his action.

So certain was the lad of this that he moved around the trunk, so as to place himself directly in the range of the warrior, provided he retained his former place. No shot, however, was fired—proof that our young friend's supposition was right — though, glance whithersoever he would, he was unable, in the gloom of the wood, to detect the faint wreath of smoke that in the sunlight would have told him the lurking place of his enemy and opened the way for a rush upon him before he could reload.

CHAPTER V

A MASTER AND TWO PUPILS

IT was at this critical juncture that Arthur Oakland was thrilled by a sound that was as unexpected as the "crack of doom."

It was not a cry or shout, but a clear, tremulous whistle, that rang out with penetrating power, its peculiarity being that the blasts were short and were repeated three times,—a peculiarity so marked indeed as to identify the signal beyond the possibility of mistake.

It was the call which Stanton Bothwell and he used when hailing each other in the woods. His cousin had arrived on the scene, and it will be admitted that no coming could have been more opportune.

Had there been any doubt in the mind of Arthur it was removed by an indistinct view of the lad approaching among the trees. Then occurred this curious conversation, every word of which was shouted and passed over the head of their enemy, crouching somewhere between them.

"Look out, Stant! There's an Indian near us!"

"I don't see him; where is he?"

Stanton stopped, gun in hand and irresolute, not knowing whether to retreat, advance, or take to cover.

"I'm trying to find out, but can't."

"Did you miss him just now?"

"It was he who fired at me?"

"Did he hit you?"

"He came mighty near it; I have n't all the bark out of my eyes yet."

"I heard a gun a little while ago."

"That was *his* gun too."

"Bah! if he can't shoot better than that, we'll get him; where do you *think* he is, Art?"

"Among those bowlders a little to the left of where you are standing, and between you and me."

"He's had time to scrooch, and I guess I'll take to cover," was the prudent decision of young Bothwell, who whisked behind the nearest tree. Since neither could precisely locate the Indian, the boys exchanged a few more words.

"How comes it you are here, Stant?" asked Arthur; "did n't you see my signal fire?"

"Yes, but you were so long on the road, I feared something had happened and I started to meet you."

"Well, something *has* happened; I stopped to

talk with some hunters that have started on a long tramp with Christopher Gist and a young Virginian that they call Major George Washington."

"Never heard of him."

"Nor did I before, but he's a splendid-looking fellow, and I guess Gist thinks he'll be able to make something of him; but, I say, Stant, father sent me to tell your folks they must come into Warrenburg, for times are squally."

"Nobody is at home but Aunt Cynthia."

"Where's your father?"

"He went off on a hunt this morning and may not be back for two or three days."

"I hope he won't be gone that long."

"But, Art, we can't keep this business up all night——"

Such evidently was the opinion of the Indian chiefly concerned, for, before Stanton Bothwell could complete his sentence, a third report rang out, the bullet this time being sent in his direction, the redskin having so shifted his position that the boy was fully exposed to his aim; but, strange as it may seem, he was not harmed, though the leaden messenger could not have passed closer without hitting him.

Both lads saw the flash, and it was proof of their fine training in wood lore that they leaped from behind their trees at the same moment.

"Quick!" called Stanton; "we'll get him before he can reload!"

They ran with headlong haste and were at the spot whence came the shot before the marksman could have rammed a new bullet home, but, quick as they were, and with the eyes of the two never once removed from the sheltering tree trunk, the Indian managed to elude them, vanishing with a skill that was inexplainable.

The boys stared at each other in blank amazement.

"Art," said his cousin, *"that Indian is n't trying to hit us!"*

"No; he could n't have missed three times like that unless he did it on purpose."

Both started for through the stillness of the gloomy wood they heard a soft laugh, coming from the point opposite where they supposed the redskin to be, and, glancing thither, they saw the figure of a tall, finely formed warrior coming toward them.

It was he who had laughed, and who now laughed again, with an odd, chuckling sound, as he walked forward, without the least evidence of misgiving.

"How do you do, brothers?" he asked in a soft, pleasing voice.

"By gracious!" exclaimed Arthur Oakland, "it's Logan!"

The Indian alluded to was in the costume common on the border a century and a half ago, consisting of hunting-shirt, leggings, ornamentally fringed and beaded moccasins, with no head-dress, excepting three stained eagle feathers, while his long, coarse, black hair dangled loosely about his shoulders, instead of displaying the defiant scalp-lock in which many of his brethren took delight. It need hardly be added that he carried powder-horn and bullet-pouch, in addition to his long, formidable rifle, and in the sash which encircled his waist were a hunting-knife and tomahawk, in the use of which he was never known to have a superior, while, despite the exhibition just made, he was equally skilful with his rifle.

"Logan the Mingo" is an historical character, whose career was one of the most striking of the many recorded in the annals of the border. The exact date of his birth is unknown, but it was probably about 1730. He was the son of Shikellany, chief of the Cayugas, and his Indian name was Tah-gah-jute, but he was given the English one of John Logan, taken from James Logan, the secretary of William Penn, who was a warm friend of the Indians throughout his life and held in affectionate remembrance by them.

Logan spent his boyhood upon Shamokin Creek, near the Moravian settlement, and was peaceably disposed toward the whites. As he grew to manhood he developed many admirable qualities. He was truthful, chivalrous, personally brave, and affable of manner. It is said that he was one of the handsomest Indians of whom we have record, his physical proportions and features being perfect.

His voice was musical and pleasing, and at times (as in the incident just narrated) he displayed a tendency to humor, quite unusual with his race. He was popular among the white people, for he had every quality to make him so. He was a wonderful runner, and, as has been intimated, none could surpass him in throwing the tomahawk or in the handling of his rifle.

While a young warrior, he was fond of roaming through Pennsylvania and Virginia, and none was so widely known on the frontiers of both colonies (and afterwards States) as he. Thomas Jefferson devoted considerable space to him in his *Notes on Virginia*, and his memorable speech, which is authentic, was one of the principal orations that were spoken by our grandfathers, when they were boys at school. The woful occurrences which gave rise to that speech, as well as the more tragic incidents of his career, took place long after the incidents we are now describing, and will be referred to in the latter pages of this work.

It will be understood that when Logan came forward and, with a smile that displayed his even white teeth, shook in turn the hand of Arthur Oakland

and Stanton Bothwell, he was in his young manhood and without a superior as a warrior. He had sat at the board of the fathers of the boys and of other settlers and was a welcome visitor at Fort Dinwiddie and other blockhouses, for he came as the friend of the white men and he always "spoke with a single tongue."

But that sagacious woodman, Christopher Gist, the comrade of young Washington, and a man whose knowledge of the American race could not be excelled, once summed up the character of Logan in his terse and accurate fashion:

"He 's an Injin through and through! We have n't a better friend between the Atlantic and the Alleghanies, but he won't always be so. 'Cause why? Some white scamp will insult him or commit an outrage against him or his friends, for that 's the way with our people; they 've done it ever since Jamestown was settled and they 'll keep it up to the end and we 'll sup sorrow for the same.

"It 'll come with Logan, and when it does the fur will fly! He 'll be forty painters rolled into one. He 's got the temper of Satan when it 's roused. I 've had some purty tough tussles in my time with redskins, and carry scars from my head to my feet. More than once I made up my mind that Kit Gist's time to go under had come, but I squeaked through and reckon I 'm good for a few more of the same sort; but, knowing what I do, if I had my ch'ice of going through the same agin, or pitching into a reg'lar, no-let-up fight with Logan, I would n't bother Logan.

" 'Cause why? He 's as quick as chain lightning, strong as a horse, can run down any deer or buck, can hit a fly on a man's nose with a rifle ball at a hundred paces, and as for that tomahawk of his, I don't b'lieve he could miss a man at fifty paces if he tried. I never seen him handle that knife, but I 'm sure he 's as handy with it as he is with his gun and tomahawk.

"Then he is n't afeard of anything that travels on two or four legs. He 's as gentle as a woman, *but don't make him mad!* I 've seen the fire, once or twice, in them black eyes of his, and I was glad it was n't me that kindled it."

Such was the homely description of Logan the Mingo, who, having had his little joke with Arthur Oakland and Stanton Bothwell, now walked smilingly forward and shook hands with them.

CHAPTER VI

THREE OLD FRIENDS

LOGAN had spent so much of his life among and in close contact with the whites that he spoke English as if he had no knowledge of any other tongue. He occasionally indulged in the metaphors peculiar to his race, but generally was as practical in his speech as those with whom he conversed.

Any one witnessing the meeting between him and the two boys would have noted the warm friendship felt by him and them toward one another. Having shaken hands, the three stood in the gathering gloom of the wood, talking like brothers.

"Where is that bearskin with which you fooled me?" asked Arthur Oakland.

"I threw it aside; I did not wish to frighten you any more."

"I was n't scared, but I wondered that the bear did not show more of himself when he came out on the bluff."

"Then you would have seen it was no bear."

"But I came near shooting at it as it was; you

saw me aim my gun and it would have been bad for you if I fired at the head that covered *your* head."

"Maybe it would," replied the Indian indifferently, "but I held the skin a little in front of my face, so that a bullet through the head would not have harmed me."

"Gracious, Logan!" exclaimed Stanton Bothwell; "you ran a frightful risk; suppose Art had aimed just back of the foreleg, which you know is a good place to shoot any animal? What then?"

"That part was covered by the trunk of a small pine."

"All the same you were dangerously exposed if he *had* fired at all."

"The current ran fast—he could not make a good aim."

The more Logan explained his course in this incident, the more reckless did it seem. It looked as if he had based all his doings upon Arthur's inability to fire truly, owing to the rough handling of his canoe by the swift current. That this calculation was correct has been proved by our account of the incident, but none the less it was a piece of foolhardiness for which it is difficult to find excuse.

"It strikes me, too," added Arthur, "that your shots came mighty near hitting me."

"But they *missed*," said the Cayuga, with a grin

that displayed a set of teeth a princess might have envied.

Let me add at this point that Logan, although a Cayuga by birth, is always referred to as a Mingo, for the reason that, while comparatively a young man, he was elected a chief of the Mingo tribe, on account of his daring and high character.

"It would n't have done for either to have come closer," said Arthur; "my eyes still smart from the bark your second bullet chipped off in front of my face."

"And I felt the wind of the ball that passed my cheek," added Stanton.

"But they *missed*," repeated Logan, still smiling.

"And of course you did it on purpose. Now, I want to ask whether I did right," said Arthur earnestly, "when I dashed out from behind the tree and tried to run you down before you could reload."

"No," was the prompt reply of the warrior.

"Why not? If I had seen you, you would have been at my mercy."

"But you did n't see me."

"How was it you dodged out of sight so quickly?"

"I dropped on my face and hurried to one side; my only fear was that you would hear me laugh."

"You say I did wrong in running toward you as I did: what should I have done?"

"Cried out as if hit and fallen to the ground, that

I might have been tempted to run forward to gain your scalp."

"Would you have done so?"

"No."

"Then what had I to gain by such a trick?"

"You did n't know I was Logan."

"Suppose it had been some one else?"

"He would not have waited to reload his gun, but would have run out and you could have shot him the next minute."

"Then, believing as I did, that it was an enemy instead of a friend, and that the fight was to the death, I did right?"

"I have shown you that you did not," persisted Logan; "if it had been some one else, he had the same chance as I to slip off to one side, and he would have had all the time he wanted to shoot you from the rear, for you did n't know where I was."

By this time it began to dawn upon both boys that, although they possessed considerable knowledge of the woods, they were children indeed before this master, who had simply amused himself at their expense, taking what appeared to be fatal risks, and yet justifying his course by the incontestable fact that he had not been scratched or even fired at.

As to his own opportunities, it will be seen that he had any number of chances to shoot down each boy at his leisure. He caused an involuntary shiver on the part of Arthur Oakland by reminding him that he was repeatedly near enough to bury his tomahawk in his brain, without giving him a moment's warning.

As if he did not wish to hurt the feelings of the youth, Logan added:

"My son did well, when he read the meaning of my footprints in the soft ground; I placed them there to see whether he would read them aright."

"How could I fail to do it?" asked Arthur disgustedly; "there was nothing in *that*."

"How did *I* act when I bounced down on the scene?" inquired Stanton.

"Like a fool," was the blunt reply.

"Why?"

"Because you did n't know any better; you stood right there where I could have shot you with my eyes shut."

"But I sprang behind a tree before you had your rifle reloaded."

"No; I could have killed you; you showed no sense, nor did Arthur, because he did not warn you against it."

"It begins to look as if you are right," observed young Oakland, who, like his cousin, could not lessen his admiration and attachment for this remarkable Indian. "I half suspected that on going to where I had left my canoe, I should find it missing."

"So you would," was the startling remark.

"I should! Where is it?"

"Let us see whether we can find it."

As he spoke, Logan led the way out of the wood and in the direction of the stream, which it will be remembered was but a short distance off. The boys followed him in Indian file, and so straight did he go that he reached the bank at the very spot where Arthur Oakland had stepped out of his canoe and drawn it up the bank.

But, as their dusky friend had intimated, it was not there, nor did the searching glances cast around them bring it to light.

"I know who the thief was," remarked Arthur significantly.

"What do you think he did with it?"

"Shoved it free, and if it has n't caught against the bank, it is several miles down-stream by this time."

"Look there," said Logan, pointing up the bank among the undergrowth.

Both lads walked the few paces necessary, and then came upon the boat nestling among the underbrush. Logan had simply hidden it there in indulgence of the humorous whim which, as has been shown, sometimes controlled his actions.

By that time, night had fully come, but the round full moon was in the cloudless sky and made everything not in shadow almost as light as at midday. The wooded bluffs on the opposite bank stood out in bold relief, and the limbs, rocks, and smaller objects could be traced with distinctness. Looking upstream, the bend a couple of hundred yards above was perceptible, as well as the green, writhing current, whitened here and there by the foam made by dashing around rocks and obstructions, and which looked like tumbled snow.

Although the canoe was buoyant enough to carry four persons of ordinary weight, it sank almost to the gunwales, when the three friends seated themselves in it.

Arthur, being the owner of the boat, naturally took up the paddle and placed himself in the middle, with his cousin in front, while Logan sat in the stern, his companions noting that he placed his rifle across his knees, with his right hand grasping it just back of the lock. Thus the weapon was ready for instant use. All three faced up-stream, for such was the proper position.

It will be remembered that the remaining part of the voyage was brief. The creek rapidly narrowed, and the current became so powerful that it would soon be impossible to make headway against it. With the unusual load, it was hard for the youth to keep the craft going at a moderate speed, but he did it manfully.

"My son paddles well," remarked the Indian, after they were fairly under way.

"But not so well as Logan does."

"My son is a child; when he becomes a man, he will do *almost* as well as I."

The boys smiled. Their friend was not only a master of woodcraft and all pertaining thereto, but none was more aware of it than himself.

"When you become tired, I'll take your place," said Stanton.

"Thank you; I will not need your help," replied Arthur.

"Look out! here's a rock right in front!"

"I know it."

With admirable skill, Arthur swung the craft around the obstruction; clearing it by a few inches, and they had begun turning the bend of the stream, when Logan uttered a guarded exclamation. He had descried something, and his two young friends made the discovery at the same moment.

CHAPTER VII

LAME PANTHER AND LOGAN

ON a rock projecting fully a rod into the stream, and elevated only two or three feet above its surface, stood an Indian warrior, who naturally saw the canoe and its occupants as soon as they observed him. He was on the left bank, and in passing him, the boat, owing to the straitness of the creek, must do so at a distance of little more than fifty feet.

The vivid moonlight brought out all the details of the figure with striking distinctness. The Indian was fully six feet in height, and his dress was similar to that of Logan, except that he displayed the taunting scalp-lock, which, as I have said, was a favorite custom among the American Indians a century and more ago. The coarse black hair was drawn up from every portion of the head, and tied tightly with a deer sinew above the crown, the upper portion dangling over, so that the hair as a whole resembled a bouquet in form. Sometimes a warrior would cut away most of the hair, except on the upper portion of the head, thus accentuating the scalp-lock, and virtually saying to all enemies: "Here is the trophy! Come and take it if you can!"

The pose of the Indian was impressive. The left foot was slightly advanced, the main weight of the body resting on the other. He stood as straight as an arrow, his right hand grasping the barrel of his rifle, whose great length brought the muzzle almost to his shoulder, with the stock resting on the rock beside his feet. Thus its appearance suggested a staff, which, however, yielded no support, since none was required.

So powerful was the moonlight that the stern countenance was clearly revealed, with its aquiline nose, prominent cheek-bones, broad mouth, and hard contour. The lines, which would have shown the Indian to be in middle life, were hidden under black, red, and yellow splotches of paint, which seemed to have been daubed upon the countenance less to proclaim that the savage was on the war-path than to give the last degree of hideousness to his features—an effort which the rings, circles, and lines made an eminent success.

"Do you know him?" asked Arthur over his shoulder, still plying his paddle vigorously.

"He is Lame Panther, chief of the Nippinocks."

"I never heard of him."

The Mingo (as we shall call him henceforward,

LAME PANTHER

though he was not yet entitled to the name) made no reply, but his left hand gently closed in front of the lock of his rifle, which was thus firmly grasped by both hands, and he never once removed his eyes from the Nippinock chieftain, whom it was evident he distrusted.

A minute later the Indian called in his own tongue, which was plainly understood by the Mingo:

"Why is Logan in the canoe with the palefaces?"

"They are his friends."

"Bring them ashore to the feet of Lame Panther."

"Logan cannot do that, but he will come himself."

"Lame Panther commands him to do as he is bidden."

The space was too great for the Nippinock to see the ominous gleam in the eyes of the Mingo, who was still closely watching him. The rifle was lifted an inch from the dusky knees, and a couple of clicks showed that the hammer had been drawn back to its full extent—but the reply was in as even a voice as before.

"Logan takes no command from Lame Panther or any of his people."

Ordinarily this would have brought an instant shot from Lame Panther, but it is probable he noted the readiness of the Mingo, and knew that if he raised his own weapon, the other would anticipate him by a second or two — enough to decide the dispute between them beyond any peradventure.

Before the Nippinock could add anything to his words, Logan said in an undertone to Arthur:

"Run the canoe to shore, and then make haste to your home."

The regular landing-point was still some distance up-stream, but it was a matter of no importance, and without a question, young Oakland swung the head of the craft to the right and drove its nose a few inches up the shingle.

"Hurry home and wait for me," added the Mingo.

It was during these brief moments that Logan was all alertness. He did not even look at the boys while addressing them nor while they were obeying his orders, but kept his gaze upon Lame Panther with his own rifle raised another inch.

Now, however, came a still more trying interval, for, in order to carry out his promise, he must needs lay down his weapon and take up the paddle. He did not remove his gun from its position, but, instead of resting on his knees, it lay across the gunwales, the stock projecting to the right and the muzzle to the left, the rifle not lying at right angles, but diagonally, so that neither end was in the way of the paddle swinging over it.

If this did not give the advantage to the Nippinock, it certainly evened matters, for it surely was as much work for Logan to drop his paddle and use his gun as it was for Lame Panther to aim and fire his weapon.

The boys would have preferred to wait on the shore and witness this meeting, which was sure to be a decisive one. They even questioned whether they might not be able to give assistance to their friend, but they held him in too high regard to disobey his unmistakable order, and, with only a few seconds' hesitation, they turned their back on the scene, and going up-stream until they struck the familiar trail, moved along that in the direction of the home of Stanton Bothwell.

As has been stated, the creek was narrow at the point where Lame Panther stood, and it took the Mingo but a minute or two to drive the canoe across it. The cunning fellow, instead of making directly for the Nippinock, landed several yards above him. He knew better than to place himself under that towering figure, which would have seized the advantage with lightning-like quickness.

From this it is not to be surmised that Lame Panther was in the least a coward. He was a desperate Indian, and was the hero of some of the most sanguinary encounters that ever took place on the border. The slight lameness which he showed when walking, though it did not handicap him in the least, was the memento of what was perhaps the most terrific fight in which Christopher Gist ever engaged with a redskin, and which he always referred to as the narrowest escape of his stormy and adventurous life.

But Lame Panther never willingly gave any favor to an antagonist. He did not fear Logan the Mingo, though he knew he was a wonderful fighter, but he was simply prudent in his action toward him.

Seeing that he had given the canoe sufficient impetus, the Mingo caught up his rifle and leaped to land ahead of the craft, managing all the time to keep the Nippinock in his field of vision. The latter came down from his elevated station and met Logan on the level ground, half-way.

"My brother, Lame Panther, is on the war-path," said Logan.

"And my brother, Logan, should be on the war-path," was the stern reply.

"Logan is the friend of the white man."

"Why is he their friend?" asked the other scornfully.

"Because they are his friends; they do him no ill."

"But before another moon they will harm him."

"When they do, Logan will dig up the hatchet and take the war-path; but Lame Panther is alone; his warriors do not go with him."

This was a shrewd effort on the part of the Mingo

to gain important information and it succeeded. The chief made haste to answer:

"Lame Panther is not afraid to take the war-trail alone, but his warriors leap at the sound of his voice, and are eager to follow him. The Nippinocks are fewer than the Iroquois or the Cayugas, but they are braver. Their men number more than a hundred, and they are all in the forest. Some have gone toward the settlements to the north, and the others are encamped in the woods yonder, waiting for their chief to return and give them his commands."

As he spoke, Lame Panther pointed directly behind him into the gloomy forest to the southward."

"The village of the Nippinocks is a long way off —a full run."

"But the war-party is nigh."

It was Logan's turn to sneer.

"The Nippinocks can do nothing; they will flee when the palefaces appear before them."

The black eyes of the chieftain flashed.

"Logan's heart is a squaw's; he is afraid."

"Will you attack Fort Dinwiddie?" was asked in the same scornful manner.

"The fort of the white men shall be laid in ashes; their scalps and the scalps of the women and children will hang from the ridge-poles of the Nippinock wigwams. Then the warriors of the other tribes shall awake and spring to their feet; their great friend from over the water will arouse and send his men, who are like the leaves on the trees, to help their red brothers, and all the palefaces shall be driven into the sea."

This was an allusion to the king of France, who was expected to aid the Indians against the English and Americans. That he did so is an historical fact, as my readers well know, for, be it remembered, it was the eve of the opening of the French and Indian War, and within the following few months occurred the appalling Braddock massacre.

It is strange how well the political situation was understood, months before hostilities, by the Indians, who were destined to play so leading a part in it that their name will always form a portion of the title of the war itself. Logan the Mingo was as intelligently informed as the Nippinock, and was about to reply in the usual boasting strain of his people when he was stopped by the words of Lame Panther.

"Logan must go with Lame Panther to fight the palefaces, for it is the command of the chieftain."

"And Logan tells him as he told him a few minutes ago, that he takes no command from Lame Panther nor from any one else."

"Then Logan is a dog and a coward!"

The two men laid hands on their knives at the same moment.

"It is Lame Panther who is the dog and coward and Logan defies him to his face."

"Does he refuse to go with the brave Nippinocks to slay the white men?"

"He does."

"Then die, dog!" thundered Lame Panther, dropping his rifle, snatching out his knife, and leaping like the animal whose name he bore at the Mingo. The latter was not an instant behind him in casting his gun aside and whipping out the weapon that at close quarters was the most deadly of all.

The chieftain was the more powerful and experienced, and enough has been said to prove he was a formidable antagonist. He was the worst kind of dusky desperado and his arm was nerved by fierce and ferocious hatred; but Logan was the more agile, skilful, and self-possessed. He fought with the wily coolness of the victor of a hundred battles. The knives clashed and spit out fire; the viciously driven weapons whizzed through vacancy, and occasionally one of them found its mark and was fleshed in the dusky body at which it was aimed.

Round and round they circled, now advancing, then retreating, the serpent-like eyes never once removed from their mutual glare, the swarthy arms darting back and forth and lunging here and there, like the flitting of birds' wings and faster it would seem than human vision could follow. The blades rasped together, and the sparks flew as from the contact of flint and steel, and still they panted and fought.

But sooner than would be supposed, the end came. The two combatants suddenly went down, there was another brief, furious struggle, and one form lay still and the other calmly rose to its feet—and the latter was Logan the Mingo, and there was not so much as a scratch on his body.

CHAPTER VIII

A DEFIANCE

WHEN Logan parted company with Arthur Oakland and Stanton Bothwell, he let them know that he expected to join them at the home of the latter, but instead of setting out to do so, he now turned in the opposite direction and plunged deeper into the woods.

He had learned from Lame Panther that a war-party of Nippinocks were in camp at no great distance and his purpose was to visit them. Taking the direction indicated by the gesture of the chieftain, he was confident that he would not have to journey far, for it was not reasonable to suppose that Lame Panther would go any great distance from his warriors at such a time, and why he had left them at all it was hard to guess.

With his wonderfully trained sense of hearing and seeing, it was impossible for the Mingo to go astray. He had penetrated barely an eighth of a mile, when the starlike twinkle of a point of light showed him he was drawing near the camp which was his destination. He strode straight forward until he gained a fair view of the scene.

Lame Panther had not exaggerated when he declared that many of his warriors had assembled near and all were eager for him to lead them on the wartrail. Fully sixty were grouped around a large fire, burning in a small natural clearing. They had partaken of venison a short time before, and were now lolling about in different attitudes, many smoking their long-stemmed pipes, some seated on the ground, others upon a fallen tree, while a number were passing aimlessly back and forth and here and there, as if they had no object in mind except to kill time.

An ordinary observer would have said that their manner and conduct was much the same as so many white men under similar conditions, but the trained eye of the dusky watcher saw a great deal more. All of these Nippinocks were in war-paint; they were armed with rifles, tomahawks, and knives, and there was an air of subdued excitement among them which indicated plainly that they believed they were on the edge of important events.

Suddenly a warrior seated on the prostrate tree sprang to his feet, raised his hand in a forceful gesture, and in a loud voice summoned his brothers to come forward. All turned their faces in his direction and then there was a general converging of

A Defiance 63

men until the entire party was grouped around him.

Standing on the log, the speaker was elevated head and shoulders above the others. Directly in front of him burned the camp-fire, so near that the passage was open for the rays, which lit up his face and features as they fell upon them. He, as a matter of course, was in war-paint, but at the first glance cast upon his stern, impassioned countenance, Logan recognized him as Leaping Deer, the well-known orator of his tribe. It was plain he was anxious to "make a few remarks."

"My brothers," he called in clear, ringing tones, "the Nippinocks have dug up the hatchet! They have gone upon the war-trail! When the palefaces hear their shouts among the forest arches, they will tremble with fear! They will run into their log wigwams and try to hide themselves from the anger of the red men!

"But, brothers, they cannot escape our vengeance! The Great Spirit loves his red children, and frowns upon the palefaces! They came across the Great Water in their canoes that had wings; they drove our fathers from their hunting grounds; when our fathers resisted they shot them down and killed their squaws and papooses.

"Brothers! the Great Spirit loves his red children, for they do his will. He has spoken in their ears and bade them take the war-trail; he has promised to help them and the palefaces shall be driven into the Great Water!

"Brothers! our father across the Great Water will send his warriors, who are like the leaves on the trees and the stars in the sky, and they will join us to slay the children of the other father, who stole away our hunting grounds and killed our squaws and papooses.

"Brothers, the children of our good father have built many homes in the valley of the Great River [Mississippi]; they are coming this way and will drive the children of our bad father into the Great Water and all shall be drowned!

"Brothers, Lame Panther, our chief, shall lead us against the strong house of the palefaces [Fort Dinwiddie at Warrenburg]! We will burn it to the ground and tear away the scalps of the palefaces, who will cry out with fear and try to hide when they hear the tramp of the Nippinocks in the woods.

"Brothers! The red men shall come from the rising and setting sun! They shall come from the home of the snow and ice and from the land that sees no snow and ice! All of them will spring from the ground, for it is the voice of the Great Spirit that is shouted in their ears, and they will heed it. Too long have we slumbered! Brothers, **awake!** awake' awake!"

The words rang out like a trumpet, and the frenzied listeners responded with frenzied cheers and the brandishing of their weapons. They were wrought to a high pitch of excitement, and had the opportunity for an attack upon the palefaces presented itself just then they would have "rushed to death as to a festival."

Not a word of this impassioned address escaped the ear of the listening Mingo. At its opening, he walked quietly forward, unnoticed in the whirlwind of emotion, and with little difficulty edged his way between the warriors, until he stood directly in front of the speaker, from whom he partly excluded the firelight.

Logan kept his eyes immovably upon the glowing countenance of Leaping Deer until he finished. Then while the fierce shouts filled the air, and the swarthy arms were flung to and fro, he stepped up beside the orator who had aroused this tempest of emotion, and who with flaming eyes and ecstatic pleasure was looking upon the work of his genius.

Leaping Deer turned upon the intruder, and recognizing Logan, surveyed him with wonder, but with no enmity, for he knew of no cause for such feeling.

The Mingo calmly looked out upon the surging waves of excitement until they had partly subsided, when he raised his hand to signify that he would say a few words. There was hardly a warrior to whom the Mingo, even at that early age, was unknown. They recognized him as a well-known friend of the whites, and were curious to learn why he appeared among them at this time. Some believed he had come to plead for peace; more supposed he had been won over by the eloquence of Leaping Deer; a few were in doubt, and all were so curious to hear his words that a profound hush quickly settled over the turbulent horde, which was quick to respond to the fervid appeals of oratory.

He began in a moderate voice, but with so clear a tone that not a syllable was lost upon his listeners.

"Brothers! we have listened to the words of Leaping Deer, and they have made your hearts glad. My brother speaks with a tongue of fire, but his words are not wise! His eyes are closed and he does not see the briars in the path before his feet!"

These few sentences clearly foretold the sentiments that were coming. That they were displeasing to the auditors was shown by the expression of their faces, their murmurs, and their gestures of dissent. Logan expected all this, but it affected him not, and he began firing his hot shot.

"Brothers! it may be as my brother Leaping Deer says that the French father will send his children across the Great Water to help the red men to drive away the children of them that stole the hunting grounds from our fathers.

"But, brothers, are you blind that you do not see that if the French gain the victory, they will take the hunting grounds from the English and keep them for themselves? Be not deceived! That is what the French will do if they prove the stronger."

The signs of dissent grew more marked. There were shouts of disapproval, and several on the outer edge of the swarm uttered threats against the "foreigner" who had dared say such unpleasant words to them. But more unpleasant ones were coming.

"Brothers! If the French are like the leaves on the trees and the stars in the sky, the English are as the sands on the seashore. They will join their brothers in the land of the Indian, and by and by there will be no Frenchmen anywhere! The strong houses that they have built along the Great River, from the snows of the north to the sleeping waters in the south, shall be turned to ashes! The Frenchmen will leap into the Great River and hide under the water to escape the wrath of the Englishmen!"

Every listener was angry, and Leaping Deer, still standing beside the Mingo on the log, exclaimed: "Logan speaks with a double tongue! he lies!"

The Mingo raised his hand as an appeal for silence, and the angry storm was partly lulled for the moment.

"The words of Logan are true! He speaks with a single tongue! Leaping Deer has spoken lies! The Nippinocks are fools to be misled by him! A great war will soon sweep over the land like a fire in the autumn forest! If the Nippinocks fight with the French their wigwams will be burned and their homes made desolate!

"Brothers, hear me! Who will lead the Nippinocks to battle?"

"Lame Panther!" was shouted from twoscore throats.

"It is a lie! Lame Panther will *never* lead his warriors to battle!"

This was beyond bearing and the infuriated listeners crowded forward to lay hands upon the daring speaker, but they were stayed by his thunderous voice:

"Lame Panther is dead! Go to the banks of the small stream that lies but a little way off yonder [indicating the direction by his extended arm], and you will find his body lying where it fell less than an hour ago!

"Lame Panther was a dog, as you are dogs! He said words to Logan that cut like a knife! They fought! See! there is not a wound upon me! But Lame Panther was slain by me, and I go to warn Fort Dinwiddie that you are coming!

"Do you say Logan lies and Lame Panther is *not*

dead? Behold! there is the scalp of Lame Panther! Feast your eyes upon it! I defy you! Logan fears you not! Look upon the scalp of Lame Panther!"

CHAPTER IX

"GOOD-NIGHT, MY BROTHER"

AS Logan shouted the fearful words, he snatched the hideous trophy from his girdle and flaunted it aloft, where every eye saw it.

There were the long, black locks, which one hand of the Mingo grasped while the iron fingers of the other closed about the barrel of his rifle. The scalp was the same in appearance as their own would have been, but instinctively every warrior felt the truth of the horrifying declaration.

A hush like that of death fell upon the awed listeners. They stood spellbound, gazing upon the Mingo, who with unparalleled audacity taunted them to their very faces, and flourished aloft the reeking trophy that had been torn from the crown of Lame Panther, their great war-chief.

Louder and clearer rang the impassioned voice:

"Do you see the scalp of Lame Panther? Logan does not want it! He gives it to you!"

And with a flirt of his hand, he flung it a dozen feet away among the upturned faces, smitten with a horror that showed through their grotesque daubings of paint.

The passage between the fallen tree upon which he stood and the crackling fire was still open. Gathering his matchless muscles with catlike agility, the Mingo made a single leap of such tremendous effectiveness that it carried him entirely over the blaze into the open space beyond. Turning his head for an instant, he shouted:

"Nippinocks! dogs! squaws! papooses! Logan defies you!"

Then with the swiftness of an arrow from the bow he vanished in the depths of the forest.

With his quick disappearance, the spell that had held breathless the band of Nippinocks was lifted and for a moment or two they gave way to unrestrainable rage. They dashed to and fro and against one another in their blind fury, with frenzied cries that sounded more like the hoarse growlings of wild animals than of human beings. Then as a sense of the situation broke upon a dozen or more, they dashed into the wood in furious pursuit of him who in their eyes was an unspeakable regicide.

Others, recalling the declaration of the Mingo, turned their steps in the direction of the stream, by whose bank he warned them they would find the body of the chieftain who nevermore should lead them in battle. As if guided by fate, two of the searchers went directly to the spot, where the words of the Mingo were confirmed. The wailing cries which a moment later rang through the arches of the forest conveyed the woful tidings to the scattered Nippinocks.

The majority of these recalled that Logan had told them he would hasten to Fort Dinwiddie to warn the garrison of the intended attack upon the settlement. Their fleetest runners separated and sped like deer through the woods, each ready to give an arm or a leg for the scalp of the daring Mingo who had committed the unpardonable crime.

But the pursuit from the first was without a shadow of hope. Of all the Nippinocks, there was none so fleet of foot as the fugitive, nor was there a living warrior his superior in woodcraft. He had gained all the start he could ask, and few of the rays of vivid moonlight penetrated the shadows amid which he glided with a swift lope that he could maintain for hours without tiring.

He did not forget his notice that he was about to start for Fort Dinwiddie, on the errand named. Indeed, the words were uttered for the purpose of deceiving the Nippinocks, for he had no purpose of going thither at this time, for why should he? It has been shown that the garrison of the post was unusually strong, and, where so many scouts were continually coming and going, they could hardly fail to learn of the Nippinocks and perhaps other tribes who had taken the war-path. That garrison, small as it was in numbers, was able to stand off one or two hundred Indians indefinitely.

Not once, throughout the stirring incidents, did Logan forget the home of Winslow Bothwell, where, in the absence of the father, the two boys and their aunt were exposed to the ferocity of the red men. In truth, the latter were already between the home and the military post, and the presence of Lame Panther so near the former looked as if he meditated paying it the visit which could have but one meaning.

But Logan, after making a change in his line of flight which enabled him to dismiss all fear of his enemies, did some serious thinking caused by the question he asked himself whether after all it was not his duty to make haste to Fort Dinwiddie with news to the garrison and settlers of their danger.

He suspected that the Nippinocks, in their rage, would keep up their pursuit to Warrenburg, and, failing to overtake him, would attack the post with a daring and recklessness tenfold greater than ordinary. The scouts who were abroad would soon learn the true state of affairs, but probably not early enough to anticipate the attack of the band.

This course being conceded as probable, they would give no attention to "smaller game," like a solitary woman and two boys—at any rate not until they had bagged the larger; or, at the worst, they would send only a small party to destroy the home and its occupants. If this theory of the situation was the true one, manifestly it was his duty, as has been intimated, to carry out the scheme he had announced to the Nippinocks, but which was intended only to mislead them.

Quick to make his decision, where life hung upon a passing second, Logan turned the matter over in his mind several times without being able to form a conclusion that satisfied himself. The real trouble was that while, giving the problem a cold-blooded view, he felt he ought to lose no time in hurrying to the settlement, his affection for the imperilled family inclined him to go thither. This inclination was strengthened by his recollection of having heard several rifle shots from that direction shortly after his encounter with Lame Panther.

It is impossible to tell what decision the Mingo would have reached had he not been helped thereto by an unexpected occurrence.

He was moving slowly through the wood, without following any trail, when his keen sense of hearing told him some one was following him. He instantly paused among the shadows and listened. The same astonishing acuteness made known that, instead of being an animal, as he had suspected, it was a biped, and therefore a man.

"Good-Night, my Brother"   75

The next natural belief was that, in some accidental manner, a Nippinock had discovered him, but the Mingo wondered why he was so unguarded in his movements. Stepping beside the nearest tree, he placed his hand upon his knife, for the encounter promised to be one in which that weapon was the superior of all others.

It has been said that, owing to the lateness of the season, few leaves remained on the trees, but the thickness of the vegetation totally excluded the moonlight in most places. Enough of the rays, however, penetrated the wood at this point to reveal to the Mingo the shadowy form of a man, and the same glance which showed this showed also that he was not an Indian.

"Budd!" called Logan, in a guarded undertone.

The other abruptly halted and stared around in the gloom, as if in doubt whence came the hail. Certain of his identity, the Mingo stepped forward.

"Wal, I'll be shot!" exclaimed the fellow in a voice that showed he was pleased; "I've been tryin' to figure out whether that was you or some redskin I didn't want to see. Shake, Logan!"

The two warmly clasped hands in the gloom, for there could be no doubt that the meeting was as pleasing to the Mingo as to the white man.

The latter was the well-remembered scout, Budd Goepel, whose name is associated with some of the most stirring incidents of the Virginian frontier. He was one of the regular rangers attached to Fort Dinwiddie, and had been absent several days on a scout to the westward when, providentially, he came upon Logan, shortly after his affair with the Nippinocks. He explained that he had made a circuit of several hundred miles, and barely missed being a spectator of the scene in which Logan was the star actor.

"What did my brother learn?" inquired the latter.

"Things look dub'us, Logan,—very dub'us; the French scamps have been among the different tribes from New York clean down to lower Virginia, and they 've raised the mischief with the redskins. On that p'int, they 've always been a powerful sight smarter than us."

"How many of your brothers are at the strong house?" asked the Mingo, ignoring the last remark. The scout thought for a moment before replying:

"I 've been away fur a week and it 's hard to answer; but I don't think there 's more nor a dozen or tharabouts."

"Too bad! too bad!" repeated Logan, with apparent anxiety.

"Why, what 's up?" asked the scout in surprise.

"A Nippinock war-party are running fast to at-

"Good-Night, my Brother" 77

tack the settlement and the strong house; they will be there before the sun rises."

"How much start have they of me?"

"Almost a half-hour."

"Bah!" laughed Goepel; "I can beat 'em by more 'n an hour."

"Will you do it?" eagerly asked the Mingo.

"Do it! of course I 'll do it! why should n't I?"

"It makes the heart of Logan sing like a bird to hear the words of his brother," said the Mingo, dropping into the metaphor of his race; "now all will be well, for when they at the strong house hear that the Nippinocks are coming, they will be ready and laugh at them."

"And, Logan, what do *you* mean to do?"

"Go to the home of my brother off yonder and tell him of his danger."

"Which the same bein' so, thar ain't no use of our dallyin'. Good-night!"

"Good-night, my brother."

And the two parted company, each bound on his perilous errand of mercy.

CHAPTER X

A FEW LIVELY MINUTES

MEANWHILE, Arthur Oakland and Stanton Bothwell found themselves involved in one of the most stirring experiences of their lives.

From the stream where they had left the canoe to the cabin which was the home of Winslow Bothwell and his family was not far, the path being distinctly marked and winding through the wood, which was broken by every manner of roughness such as is found among the foothills of all important mountain ranges. It was so familiar to the boys that they would have had no trouble in making their way over it on the darkest night.

The narrowness of the path caused the full moon to be of less help than would be supposed, but as the orb was high in the sky, there were frequent turnings of the trail that were illuminated by the silvery rays.

Stanton took the lead, his rifle resting on his shoulder, while his cousin was only a few steps behind. They spoke rarely, for there was something in the situation which filled them with uneasiness. Logan had left them for the purpose of meeting the war-chief of the Nippinocks, and his manner and words foreshadowed the encounter which, as we have learned, really took place.

There was no misgiving as to the Mingo, but the presence of Lame Panther so near their home and the information that had lately reached the boys filled them with vague alarm. The father of Stanton had gone off on a hunt which would probably last two or three days. Aunt Cynthia, therefore, was alone. This had happened several times before, and the strong-minded woman had had no objection. Indeed, she had expressed herself relieved now and then to be rid of the presence of father and son, inasmuch as it gave her a better opportunity to "clean up" and fix things about the house.

But the situation was now very different, when a tangible peril impended over the home and she knew nothing of it.

The youths had passed over a third of the intervening distance, both silent and stepping lightly, when Arthur suddenly exclaimed in an undertone:

"Stant, somebody is following us!"

Both stopped abruptly and listened. Two or three footfalls were heard, from some near point behind them, but just beyond the bend, and then they ceased. The pursuer had become aware of the halt and he also halted. There could be no mistake as to his presence, and the boys whispered together.

"I don't like the idea of having an Indian sneaking along at my heels," said Arthur, "with the chance of taking a crack at me with his rifle or hurling his tomahawk, when I 'm not looking."

"I should n't fancy it either, but I don't see how we 're going to help it; he has stopped because we stopped and he won't give us a chance to hurt him."

"I can fix it," said Arthur, sinking his voice still lower; "when he hears us moving ahead again, he will start up; I 'll step to one side and wait for him to pass; then I 'll slip in behind him and we 'll have him between us, and we 'll do as we please with him."

"Unless he 's smart enough to do as he pleases with us; suppose there are two or three of them?"

"They will make a lively fight, and I guess we had better sneak off home while we have the chance."

The scheme was a daring one, but it was carried out at once. Arthur moved as stealthily as a shadow over a space of a couple of yards, where he felt safe in taking his position in the gloom beside the trunk of a tree that was of less diameter than his body. Although there was little or no moonlight in the path, he was confident of being able to catch the outlines of one or more warriors as they slipped past.

Stanton immediately resumed his walk, taking care that his footsteps were a little heavier than usual. Almost at the same moment, the faint sounds from the rear showed that his pursuer was again in motion.

Arthur gently raised the hammer of his rifle and kept on the alert.

"There seems to be only one, and I'll pick him off as soon as he comes in range," was his grim thought, as he held himself ready to act.

But an amazing fact became apparent within the next second or two. The keen ear of Arthur heard the soft footfalls drawing rapidly nearer, and he stood in the expectation of firing the deadly shot, when he became aware that the Indian had passed the point and was hurrying after Stanton Bothwell!

"How the mischief did he do *that*, without my seeing him?" the chagrined youth asked himself.

The explanation which instantly suggested itself was that the redskin suspected the truth, and had crouched so low that his head and shoulders were below the youth's line of vision while passing the point where he was on the lookout.

Arthur quickly regained his wits, and, alarmed for the safety of his cousin, cautiously stepped back into the trail. He had learned there was but one pursuer, who was now between the two. True, upon the discovery of his danger, he could leap aside, but the watchful Arthur believed that in the event of the warrior's making the attempt, he could wing him on the fly.

An extraordinary situation came to the relief of the boy. The course of the trail was such that for a distance of several rods the moonlight fell full upon it. Throughout this space, the path led steadily upward. Stanton Bothwell had just passed the summit and was descending the other side. His cousin saw his head and shoulders sinking from view, as if they were going down into the ground, but, as they were doing so, the pursuer was passing up the slope and coming into plain sight.

Indeed he was so near that Arthur Oakland felt it useless to decrease the distance. Waiting until the enemy was plainly seen and with the moonbeams gleaming on the sights of his rifle, he took deliberate aim at the foe, who had not discovered the peril behind him, and pulled the trigger.

And what is more, he struck him fairly, but it was not an Indian but a panther, which was trying to sneak up behind the boys and leap upon the shoulders of the nearer and rend him to pieces. Firing from the rear, Arthur buried his bullet somewhere in the animal's neck without inflicting a mortal hurt.

A Few Lively Minutes 83

With the body of the panther sloping upward, in line with the ground, the brown, sinewy back was visible from the head to the slowly swaying tail. Upon receiving the bullet of Arthur Oakland, a convulsive twitch ran through the graceful and powerful figure, and, without moving in his tracks, he lashed his ribs with his tail, turned his head, and looked back to see where the shot came from.

The phosphorescent glitter of the eyes and the guttering growl from between the red, parted jaws showed that all the fury of the brute, whose kind was among the most frightful denizens of the forests of the Atlantic slope, was roused to the unrestrainable point.

He saw that youthful figure standing in the trail, but a little way behind him, so absorbed in viewing the result of his aim that he forgot the law that had been taught him from the moment the first firearm was placed in his hands, which was never to lose a second, after discharging his gun, in reloading it.

The panther was prompter than the boy, for, recognizing his foe, he emitted another rasping howl, and whirled about with the suddenness of lightning. Instead of walking or trotting, he advanced in a series of leaps so prodigious that three or four were sufficient to carry him to the object of his fury.

With the first glare and growl of the brute,

Arthur awoke to the fact that he had neglected to reload his gun. As it was, however, it would have availed nothing, had he made the attempt, for the interval was too brief; and it was now too late to make even a beginning.

Nor had he time to dart back into the wood and climb the limbs of a tree beyond reach of the ravening brute. Darkness and light were much the same to the fearful creature, and a flight into the wood would render his work of slaying the boy so much the easier.

Standing with one foot advanced and rifle clubbed, with the stock drawn back over his shoulder, the youth had barely time to brace himself for the assault, which was made the next instant, with the viciousness of a cyclone.

With a coolness remarkable in one so young, Arthur waited until the panther made his last bound, and was descending the parabola that would land him upon his face and chest, when he brought down the weapon with all the power he could concentrate in his muscular arms.

It was a tremendous blow, delivered with precision, the stock crashing against the iron skull with a force that sent the beast tumbling over and over, snarling, clutching, and clawing, but leaping instantly to its feet for a second attack, with undiminished fierceness.

ARTHUR AND THE PANTHER　　　　Page 84

A Few Lively Minutes

Arthur expected it, and like a flash braced himself in the same pose as before. But it will be remembered that his cousin was at hand and he bounded up the other side of the slope and came down the incline at headlong speed. The clear moonlight revealed the situation, and, dropping on one knee, he took deliberate aim at the panther, as he was in the act of rising on his second bound.

His cousin was in the line of fire, but Stanton knew where he was aiming and at the critical moment let fly. The bullet bored its way through the brain of the beast before the body could feel the full force of the gathering muscles, and instead of descending upon or coming within reach of the youth, it dropped short several feet, rolling over, snarling, and clawing in its death agony. Arthur recoiled several paces and calmly saw the animal die, as it did within the next two or three minutes.

"Well, I guess that 's all," coolly remarked Stanton; "let 's load our guns and hurry home."

Both proceeded to do this sensible thing, when Arthur uttered an exclamation of dismay.

"My gracious! look at *that!*"

He held up his weapon as he spoke, and showed the hammer had been snapped off short by its contact with the head of the panther.

"I would n't have had that happen for a thousand

pounds," was the comment of the owner; "the gun is of no more use than a club of wood."

"It served you pretty well for a club. But old De Val at Fort Dinwiddie will soon mend it for you."

"We are not at Fort Dinwiddie yet," replied Arthur significantly. "Ah, me!" he added with a sigh; "it can't be helped; it's no use of putting a charge in the barrel, and as soon as you finish loading yours we'll go home."

Stanton quickly completed the task, and they resumed their journey in the same order as before. The distance was so brief that they speedily reached the clearing in the middle of which stood the cabin of Winslow Bothwell. A light shone from the narrow curtained window at the side of the heavy door, but afforded no glimpse of the interior. All was as quiet and apparently undisturbed as if no such thing as war or violence were known.

"I guess Aunt Cynthia has n't been bothered—"

At that moment, the door was suddenly opened and a man came out as if propelled by a catapult. As he sprawled forward on his hands and knees, the yellow candle-light within the cabin showed that the forceful motor was Aunt Cynthia!

CHAPTER XI

AUNT CYNTHIA'S ASTONISHED CALLER

IT was intimated in the opening pages that Aunt Cynthia, the maiden sister of Winslow Bothwell, was not only strong-minded, but had a temper of her own, and we shall now proceed to demonstrate the truth of the assertion.

Stanton had left the cabin only a few minutes, on that crisp autumn afternoon, to meet his laggard cousin, when the lady, while busy with her household duties, was startled by a gentle tapping on the door. She looked up in surprise, for the latchstring had not been drawn in, and it was the invariable fashion on the border, under such circumstances, to enter without any preliminary knocking.

"You big fool! why don't you pull the string and come in?" was the response of the impatient lady, uttered in a loud voice.

Thereupon the leathern thong was mildly twitched, and as the door swung inward, a man, hat in hand, bowing low, and smiling obsequiously, stepped hesitatingly across the threshold. His face was dark, and hair, eyes, and mustache were jet black in color. He was in the uniform of a captain of the French army, and wore a handsome sword at his side, and carried a fine single-barrel pistol, thrust in the crimson sash that encircled his waist.

"I hopes I find zee fine ladee well, these delightful day," he remarked, hat still in hand, and bowing so low that only the top of his bushy head was visible to one in front.

"Who are you?" demanded the astonished woman, standing in the middle of the room, with a kettle in one hand, her thin face the picture of amazement.

"I am Captain Eugene Choteau at your zarvice, my most eest-ti-ma-ble ladee," and, bringing his forehead almost to his knees, he added:

"I am ze noble ladee's slave—I does her bidding and I am zo happy!"

"None of that!" warned Aunt Cynthia, with a suggestive lifting of the utensil in her grasp; "if you belong to the French army, what are you doing in *this* part of the country?"

"I am paying my respects to the ze noblest and most beau-ti-ful ladee— I begs a zousand pardons if I have zo much as offend you once; I vill say no mores, zo it makes my heart aches."

"You 'd better not! Sit down in that chair," commanded the woman, pointing to a seat near the door; "stop acting the monkey, and talk like a sensible person."

With several genuflections, and repeated expressions of thankfulness, Captain Choteau carefully placed himself in the chair indicated, deposited his hat on the floor beside him, crossed his legs, the lower portions of which were encased in cavalry boots, and folding his hands, on one finger of which gleamed a handsome diamond ring, addressed the lady with every evidence of the profoundest respect.

"I am ze zarvint of ze great king of France; he loves ze red men of ze woods and he does me ze great honor to veesit them zat I may tell him how vell zay be. Ze good king pays me more honor zan I dezerve."

It was well for Captain Choteau that Aunt Cynthia did not grasp the whole suggestiveness of these words, for they were a confession on the part of the officer that he was a French emissary to certain tribes, and it was his business to aid in bringing the Indians to the side of the French in the mighty war that was impending.

It was nearly time for the evening meal which Aunt Cynthia was preparing. Despite the scarcity of the luxury, Winslow Bothwell generally kept his family supplied with tea, chiefly because of his sister's fondness for it. The forests afforded abundant game, the streams contained fish, and flour and sugar occasionally were brought from Fort Dinwiddie, which obtained them from some of the seacoast cities. The odor of cooking food was perceptible and Captain Choteau was a-hungered.

"I don't see what business it is of your king whether the Injins are well or ill; they don't belong to *him*," said the puzzled woman.

"Zay belongs to nobodee but zemzelves; you speaks truly, but zay trades wid ze French, who gives zem presents. Ah!" added the officer, sniffing the air, "how very delightful zat parfume smells."

"What do you mean?"

"Ze excellent food zat you are making ready for your familee."

"Are you hungry?"

"I hef eat notting zince ze sun comes up in ze sky; I was zo hungry zat I never was zo hungry."

No one ever appealed in vain to the hospitality of the Bothwell family. The fact that her strange caller was hungry awoke the sympathy of Aunt Cynthia.

"If you will do all the talking for a little while," said she, considerably mollified, "though I much prefer you should keep still till you learn English, I'll get supper ready."

"Ah, you are zo kind; I vill do nottings but

leesten and vatch and admire ze grace of ze beau-ti-ful ladee——''

Aunt Cynthia, who was moving to the fireplace, abruptly paused and turned angrily toward him. In all probability he would have suffered for his boldness, had he not been prompt to trim to the wind.

"I begs ten zousands pardons, but I know not your Engleesh well; I hope I do not offend vid my bad words; do you not speak our beau-ti-ful French?"

"No; I don't know anything about your lingo, and I wish you 'd stop talking till I get through my work."

"I vill do zo, my beau-ti— my good friend."

Captain Choteau made a brave attempt to keep his promise, but he could not help breaking out now and then into ecstatic compliments, for which he would have received something more than looks by way of reproof, but for the sympathy he had roused by declaring he was in need of food.

The simple meal was soon prepared, and it did not require a hungry man to appreciate the crisp brown venison, the light bread, the fragrant tea, and the sweet milk and butter furnished by the cow belonging to the family. Aunt Cynthia had no superior as a housekeeper and cook, and the meal could not have been surpassed, though it was just what she would have prepared for herself and nephews whom she confidently expected within the next hour.

The officer was nearly famishing, and probably had been without food longer than he said. Although he could not forget his courtesy, and tried the patience of his hostess by his effusiveness, yet he gave his main attention to his meal until it was completed.

He was too familiar with border sentiment to offer payment for the food, though he had considerable gold about his person and would have been glad to pay generously. He was sincerely grateful, but took an unfortunate way of expressing it.

The meal being ended and feeling that he must soon go, he repeated his thanks and added:

"You hef been zo kind, my good ladee, and you hef told me about your brother and your nephews, and I now tells you vid zorrow zat you must leef dis loafly home."

"Why?" sharply asked the woman, as the two shoved their chairs back from the table; "I am suited and so is my brother, and the Indians are friendly."

"But a great war is coming; ze French are building one grand empire zat reaches from Canada to ze Gulf of Mexico; ze Engleesh are great fools to zink zay can stop zem, but zay vill try to do zo."

For most of the time previous to the Revolution,

AUNT CYNTHIA AND CAPTAIN CHOUTAU   Page 95

the colonists were referred to collectively as Englishmen, and Captain Choteau thus included the subjects of Great Britain on both sides of the Atlantic. His remark gave his listener a glimmering of the truth.

"Do you mean to tell me that France can whip England and her American colonies?" she asked in a voice that betrayed her fast-rising anger.

"Un-doubted-ly, my good"——

"Why France was never able to give England alone a decent war, and with the Americans to help her, your people will be ground to powder. Have you come among the Indians to persuade them to help France in the war you say is coming?"

"Let me explain, fair ladee——"

But Aunt Cynthia had heard enough. Leaping from her chair, she seized Captain Choteau with both hands by the collar, and, despite his protests, ran him toward the door, which she opened with a quick movement of one hand, and then thrust him forth with such violence that he fell on his hands and knees. She flung his hat after him, and then slammed the door without observing that her nephews were but a few paces distant.

CHAPTER XII

WITHIN THE CABIN

ARTHUR OAKLAND and Stanton Bothwell were amazed at the sight of Captain Choteau, as he plunged out of the cabin, followed by his hat, and the banging of the door by Aunt Cynthia.

Naturally they would have been greatly frightened had not the first glimpse of the visitor shown him to be a white man. As it was, it was clear that the relations between him and the lady had become strained.

The officer had just donned his hat and begun brushing the dust from his uniform, when he perceived the two youths standing near and contemplating him. Instantly his hat went off again and he bowed low.

"I greets my young friends wiz a *bon jour*," he said, resuming his expansive grin.

"Good-evening," they replied, and it was Arthur who asked:

"Is that the way you always leave a house, monsieur?"

Within the Cabin

"Le Captain Choteau," he corrected, "at your zarvice; iz zat fine ladee your uncle?"

"No; she's our aunt," replied Stanton.

"Ah, how for-tu-nate in having so noble and beau-ti-ful a ladee for your granddaughter—I mean for ze aunt; but she is one ladee of strong impulse."

"It has that look, Captain; you must have said something that displeased her."

"Ah, no; she would give me no time to zay it; I would explain, but she hinted zat I calls some oder fine day."

"A rather strong hint, as it looked," suggested Arthur.

"Veree strong—veree strong; if she will afford me ze pleasure of giving her lessons in fencing, she will make one fine swordsladee."

"Suppose you go back with us and we have matters cleared up," said Stanton, who felt that he and his cousin were hardly acting a hospitable part.

"I zanks you veree mooch, but I will do myself zee honor to call zome oder day, when zee skies are clearer; I bids you good-evening, my grand friends."

They returned his salutation, and, amused and puzzled, watched him, as with erect, military step he strode over the path, across the clearing, taking the same route followed by themselves and disappearing in the gloom of the forest.

The perturbed Aunt Cynthia had caught the murmur of voices, and she now drew open the door to learn what it meant. Recognizing her nephews she asked sharply:

"Do you boys know you are late for supper?"

"We could n't very well help it, aunty?" gently replied Stanton, as he and his cousin entered, removed their caps, leaned their guns in the corner, and each took a chair.

"I 'm tired of excuses—always excuses; did n't I tell you and Arthur last week that the next time you were late, you should n't have a mouthful to eat?"

"My gracious! I believe you hinted something like that, but I forgot all about it," replied Stanton with affected dismay.

"It 's time you understood that when I say a thing I *mean* it," observed the good woman in the severest of tones; "I 'm tired of such goings on."

Stanton looked slyly across at his cousin and winked. Arthur returned the wink and furtively grinned. The youngsters were not scared. They were as hungry as wolves, but they knew, too, that their aunt loved them and would go without food herself to save them from hunger.

"It 's time you boys were larned a lesson," added the woman in the same vinegary manner;

"I'm sick of warning you and warning you; you know it tires me to talk and I hate it."

"What makes you talk so much, then, aunty?" meekly inquired Stanton.

"Hush!" she said, turning so threateningly toward her nephew that he ducked his head, threw up his elbow, and nearly fell off his chair. Arthur chuckled, whereupon she wheeled toward him. His expression instantly became preternaturally solemn; he folded his hands and sat up and tried to look like a real good boy. The aunt resumed:

"Land knows it's mighty little I have to say! If folks was like me and kept a quiet tongue in their heads, there would n't be half the trouble there is in the world."

The boys noticed that plenty of good things remained on the table, and with their tremendous appetites these were mighty tempting, but they were too wise to rush things.

"I was afraid that Frenchman had eaten everything up," mildly ventured Arthur.

"Do you suppose I 'd let him do anything like *that?*" demanded Aunt Cynthia, looking so threatening, as she took a step toward Arthur, that he, too, flung up his elbow as a guard to his face and tumbled backward off his chair, with his feet kicking toward the ceiling. Stanton could not check his laughter, and even the aunt smiled at the ridiculous performance, but the smile did not last more than a tenth of a second.

Arthur, still affecting to be scared, gingerly backed upon the chair again, and seating himself on the edge, twiddled his thumbs, keeping his eye on his relative, and ready to make a dash the instant she took another step in his direction.

"La, sakes?" exclaimed Cynthia, "what under the sun is getting the matter with you? You act as if you did n't have not one bit of sense."

Arthur straightened up in his chair, gazed longingly over the feast, and gave a sigh that seemed to come from his shoes.

"I guess it 's 'cause I 'm so hungry; I feel sorter faint and queer, as if I had n't eaten anything for two weeks and a half; if I flop over in a faint, aunty, it 'll be 'cause I 'm so weak for food that I can't help it."

"Land sakes alive!" exclaimed the lady, aghast; "why did n't you tell me that before? Come right up to the table and eat all you want. How do *you* feel?" she asked, turning inquiringly toward her other hopeful nephew.

"Jes' like Art; I guess I can hold out two or three minutes longer before dying——"

"What are you waiting for? Did n't you hear me tell you both to stuff yourselves till you bust? What are you waiting for? If you don't——"

Both boys had their arms around the waist and

neck of their aunt, hugging, kissing, and mixing up their remarks:

"You 're the best aunty that ever lived! We never could get along without you! We would n't sell you for the crown of England! You dear, good thing!"

"Oh, go away with your nonsense," she replied, cuffing their ears and struggling free; but did n't she love those mischievous, manly boys? Aye, she would have borne the tortures of death unmurmuringly to keep suffering from them.

"Now, remember," she added, shaking her finger at them, as they fell to, and looking awful in her wrath, "this is the last time you 'll fool me! You can't try any more fainting tricks over me; I ain't sartin by no means that you was n't purtending. If you was—!" and she paused, compressed her lips, and shook her head.

"Honest, aunty," sputtered Stanton as well as he could with his cheeks distended with bread and meat, "we were real—hungry!"

For some reason, she did not seem to catch the dubious nature of this explanation, but kept herself busy in administering to the wants of the two youths, and it must not be supposed that it was by any means an easy task.

It may sound unreasonable to the reader that this frivolous scene should take place when both boys were aware of the danger whose shadow already rested upon the threshold; but those who live on the border become accustomed to peril, which, until it directly comes, impresses them no more than ordinary every-day occurrences.

It would be a momentous matter indeed that could hold the attention of two furiously hungry boys, before that craving was satisfied to a partial extent at least. As the cousins began to grow more comfortable, their interest in outside questions revived. The first inquiry was as to the cause of Captain Choteau's peculiar departure. It took but a few minutes for the aunt to give the particulars of all that had occurred.

"Everybody seems to agree we're close on to a big war with France," she added, "and the p'ison Injins will mix in it of course. To think that Captain Choteau set at the very table where you've eat enough for ten men, and then told me he's the agent of the king of France among them same Injins to stir 'em up to fight against our settlements! It's scandalous!"

"It *is* rather rough," replied Arthur; "I think, Stant, if we had known that we would have made him prisoner."

"We would have done it anyway, if we had n't been so weak from hunger that he could have knocked us over with a feather."

"Well, aunty," said Arthur earnestly, "it is true that we are near a great war with France; from what I have learned, most of the fighting will be to the north of us, but Kit Gist, who is on his way with a young Virginian, named George Washington, to visit one of the French officers, tells me most of the Indians will be on the side of the French, and we shall have trouble in this part of Virginia with them."

"O that scandalous villain that was here! If I had known what he was up to how I would have shook him!"

"You jarred him pretty well. We met Logan late this afternoon and he came up the creek with us."

"*He's* the most decent Injin I ever knowed."

"Well, he says what the men at Fort Dinwiddie say, that you and Uncle Winslow must n't stay here another day."

"What are we to do?"

"Go to Warrenburg till the danger is over."

"But your uncle is away and may not be back for several days."

"That need n't hinder *our* going," remarked Stanton; "he will understand when he comes back and finds us gone and will follow us."

"It may be, too, added Arthur, "that he will learn of the danger and will be here to-night or to-morrow."

"It won't do to wait for him."

At this moment, Arthur Oakland, who was looking at the door, saw the latch-string gently twitched, and, as the door swung inward, Logan the Mingo stepped silently across the threshold.

CHAPTER XIII

THE COUNCIL OF WAR

NO visitor could have been more welcome, but the first glance at the Mingo startled all three, for he was in his war-paint. His handsome countenance was daubed with circles, stripes, lines, and dots in black, red, yellow, and white. Where he had obtained the pigments was a mystery, but it may be suggested that the dead body of one of the Nippinocks—possibly that of Lame Panther—furnished the material, since it is a common practice among Indians on the war-trail to carry their paint with them, so as to renew their disfigurement when it becomes necessary.

There was no mistaking the voice of the Mingo, however, when with a smile he said:

"Good-evening, my friends."

And then, as all responded, he turned and drew in the latch-string, thus locking themselves in. Facing about again, he leaned his rifle against the wall behind the door, and still keeping his feet, looked at the table, partly spread, with an expression whose meaning could not be mistaken.

"If you 'd seen these two boys eat, Logan," exclaimed Aunt Cynthia, "you would wonder that there was a mouthful left. They 're always hungry, but I guess there 's a little for you."

She hastily rose from her chair, and replaced a goodly supply of venison that had been removed.

"There is more than Logan wishes," remarked the Mingo, as he sat down, "and he thanks his paleface friend."

It was noticeable that he confined his attention to the meat, not touching the bread and disregarding the tea, a cup of water at the conclusion of the meal serving him. He ate only a moderate quantity, and, when he was through, shoved back his chair, just as a white man would have done.

"Logan saw a painter on the trail," he said, addressing the boys inquiringly.

"Yes," replied Arthur, "we had a scrimmage with one," and he gave a brief account of the incident with which the reader is familiar.

"Too bad you broke your gun."

"Why, I did n't tell you anything about *that*," said the astonished Arthur.

The Mingo smiled and pointed to where the weapon leaned in the corner. It was the first glance they had seen him cast in that direction and yet he had noted the accident before he was in the house for five minutes.

"Let me see it," sharply commanded Aunt Cynthia, and her nephew obediently brought the weapon forth and explained the mishap, as he stood in front of her.

"Did you ever see such a careless boy?" she asked; "how did you do that?"

"By hitting the head of the painter so hard."

"What made you hit him so hard?"

"To prevent his killing me."

"Why did n't you use the other end of your gun?"

"It would n't have hurt him much."

"But would have saved your rifle."

"And lost my life."

"He is a brave boy; he did right; let me see it," said Logan.

Arthur handed the weapon to the Mingo, who examined it carefully. The hammer had been broken off close to the barrel and was lost. He shook his head and repeated his exclamation:

"Too bad! too bad! *You need the gun!*"

There was a world of meaning in the remark and all felt it.

"Old De Val at Fort Dinwiddie will soon mend it for me."

And then, strangely enough, the Mingo repeated the very words of Arthur Oakland in reply to a similar remark by his cousin earlier in the evening.

"We are not at Fort Dinwiddie yet"; and he added still more significantly, "we shall have much trouble in going there."

Logan had told his friends nothing of his stirring experience earlier in the evening. The boys were curious to know, but did not question him. He explained enough only for them to understand the situation.

"There is a war-party of the Nippinocks to the northward; there is another large party near us; they are on their way to attack Fort Dinwiddie; some of them may come *here*."

"And you are in war-paint, Logan," observed Aunt Cynthia.

"It is that Logan may go among the Nippinocks, when the sun does not shine, and they will know him not."

The boys had suspected this explanation before it was made.

"You mean," pursued the woman, "that we must not remain here?"

The Mingo bowed his head.

"When do you think we ought to go?"

"To-night."

Aunt Cynthia compressed her thin lips and shook her head decisively.

"I can't leave to-night."

"Why not?" impatiently asked Stanton.

"Because I'm not ready; I'm not going traipsing through the wood all night long; we can start early in the morning and reach Warrenburg by sundown; my mind's made up, and I don't want to hear nothing more about it."

The disgusted boys knew it was useless to argue with her, and they looked at the Mingo. He was sitting on the other side of the room, his black eyes fixed steadily upon the countenance of the stubborn woman, as if trying to read her.

It is possible that Logan was susceptible to the influence of the other sex; but, be that as it may, he now made one of the greatest mistakes of his life.

"We will wait until the light comes again in the woods, and then start for the fort, *if the Nippinocks will let us.*"

Even the grave significance of the last words was lost upon the strong-minded woman, who, if she understood them, did not allow her resolution to be affected. Her nephews were so wrought up that they would have broken into open rebellion, but for the unexpected change of front on the part of the Mingo. As it was, Stanton could not restrain the remark:

"We're in a lovely position for defence! Father is gone and Arthur's gun is broken; that leaves only two weapons, counting Logan's."

"And is n't that all you would have in the woods,

where there would be no house to protect us?" she asked, in her most peppery manner.

"Logan would keep us out of the reach of the Nippinocks."

"You don't know whether he would or not; of course he would do his best, but he can't do everything; ain't I right, Logan?"

He inclined his head.

"Let me hear no more about it," said the woman, thus closing the discussion.

Since it was agreed that the party should remain in the cabin throughout the night, it was necessary to "take an account of stock," or in other words, learn what means of defence was at the command of the defenders.

Of course, the Mingo was a host within himself. Without him, the boys and their aunt would have been in a woful situation indeed, with only a single rifle available.

The cabin was the ordinary one of logs, dovetailed at the corners, strongly built and with but a single apartment below and two above. Although, when built, the Indians for many miles around were peaceable, Winslow Bothwell followed the universal custom of providing, so far as he could, against a peril that it may be said was never wholly absent.

There was but the single puncheon door, which could be powerfully secured by massive bars until it was almost as strong as the log walls themselves. The only windows below stairs were two, one on either side of the door, and so narrow that even a boy could not force himself through them. They were provided with glass panes, which was quite a luxury in colonial days. There were no windows above, but a number of loopholes afforded the necessary light and ventilation. The roof of split logs was steeply shelving, and they had been so seasoned by wind and weather that they were readily ignitible. Since there was no trap-door, the defenders were without any means of extinguishing the flames when they had once been kindled.

The connecting stairs between the lower and upper stories was a sloping ladder in one corner. The chimney was of compactly laid stone, the mortar of which had been baked as hard as the material itself, and it formed the greater portion of one end of the cabin. The crude furniture, inclusive of the indispensable spinning-wheel, was of the simplest character, and need not be described in this place.

Inasmuch as it was necessary to provide for a stay of several days, the first step was to ascertain how well off our friends were in the way of provisions and water.

The food and material from which to prepare it were abundant enough to last for a week, or even longer by putting themselves on short allowance.

The weather was only moderately cool, and if no fuel were used except for culinary purposes, there was sufficient piled at the side of the fireplace.

But, somewhat to the surprise even of Aunt Cynthia, it was found there was substantially no water on hand. A good deal had been used in preparing tea, and it so happened that the last cupful was drunk by Logan the Mingo.

Water was more necessary than food and every one knew it.

"I will get some from the spring," said Stanton, catching up the empty pail and starting for the door, but, before he could lift the latch, the Mingo interposed.

"Let my son stay at home; Logan will go," and he took the utensil from his hand.

There was no questioning such authority, and the boys felt the significance of the warrior's action.

"Let the latch-string stay inside," were the still more significant words; "when I come, I will speak my name, and you shall open the door."

CHAPTER XIV

AN UNEXPECTED PRESENT

NOT one of the three inmates of the cabin failed to understand the ominous meaning of the Mingo's action.

It was too dangerous for either of the boys to travel alone the short distance to the spring and back. The war-party of the Nippinocks were in the neighborhood and it was not impossible that some of their scouts were reconnoitring near at hand, and were already studying from different points the defences of this lonely home in the Alleghanies. If such were the fact, it would not do for one of the white party to venture within their reach.

Stanton Bothwell sat down in his chair near the door that he might be ready to lift the latch and admit Logan the moment he presented himself. Arthur went over and placed himself beside him. Aunt Cynthia seemed to feel that as a tidy housekeeper she had allowed the "things" to remain too long on the table. She therefore began washing and cleaning the dishes and removing them to the shelves which her brother had made for her at the corner of the room near the broad fireplace, the water used being that which had been rendered unpalatable, except in an emergency that seemed now to be removed.

While thus employed, the good woman did not speak. The furtive glances which the nephews cast at her revealed an unusual expression of sternness on her thin features. The lips were firmly set and the gray eyes looked hard, as she moved about in her homespun attire, her nimble feet making no more noise than if she were "shod with silence."

"She knows she has made a dreadful mistake," said Stanton in a low voice, "but she's too stubborn to own it."

"Don't you think Logan was weak to give in to her?"

"I don't know whether he was weak or only wise. He has eaten at our table many times and *knows* aunty very well."

"She's the boss, when there's any argument going. I've no doubt Uncle Winslow thinks he runs things here, but he does n't."

"Only *me*," remarked Stanton; "he runs me pretty well."

"But she interferes at times."

"Not a bit of it! You never saw two persons agree so beautifully as they do,—that is, where I'm in it. If aunty says she thinks it is time father took me in hand, he says that is just what he was thinking, and then he stops thinking and goes to acting. If she tells him, when he comes home from your house, that she has had to box my ears, he says he wonders that she waited so long. Oh, they never have any trouble over *me*."

"All the same, Logan ought to have made her start with us to-night, and that, too, without waiting ten minutes or trying to carry anything with us."

"How would he do it?"

"Why he could have threatened to tomahawk her if she did n't mind him."

"Do you fancy *that* would have scared her? I thought you knew aunty better."

"I suppose you think she would know he did n't mean to do it."

"It would n't make any difference whether he did or not. Why, she——"

Arthur suddenly pinched the thigh of his cousin. Their relative, as she moved about the room, seemed to have caught several of their words and glanced warningly at them. As Stanton abruptly ceased, she asked in her peremptory manner:

"What is that you started to say?"

It is to be feared that the young man did not confine himself strictly to facts as he promptly made reply:

"Why, she 's the best aunty that ever lived, and

I hope she won't die for a hundred years; I am sure that if she had stopped for a minute to think, she would have made up her mind that where Indians have mixed in, the best thing to do is to take the advice of a good Indian and——"

"That 'll do! No more of *that!*" And, looking sterner than ever, the woman resumed her household work, which was soon completed.

"Good gracious!" exclaimed Stanton, taking care to sink his voice still lower, "she gets worse every day; she 's got the sharpest temper of any woman in Virginia; I don't see how father and I stand it; one of these days, we 'll both make a break and run away; she 's the dearest soul that ever lived," added the young rascal, raising his voice, but looking in the face of his cousin, as if his words were intended solely for him, "and I tell you it will be a dreadful day when we have to part."

The odd look which the aunt gave them raised an uncomfortable doubt as to whether she was wholly deceived.

But the situation was not one to inspire mirth, and the naturally light-hearted youths became thoughtful as the minutes passed.

"Is n't it time Logan got back?" asked Stanton.

In colonial times, watches were so rare that only a few carried them, and the households were scarce which contained one of those old-fashioned clocks that still retain their value. The hour-glass, the sun-dial, and marks on the window or floor were the common time-pieces. The Bothwell home had notches cut here and there, which when the sun was shining gave considerable help, but of course were useless at other times. Guess-work was the only recourse, and the reader would find it hard to credit the skill which our forefathers often attained in that respect.

"Aunty," said Arthur, "please tell me what time it is."

"It lacks a few minutes of eight o'clock."

"Thank you; should n't Logan be here?"

"No; if he was as lazy as you two boys, it would take him a half-hour to bring a pail of water; he 's at the spring now, and will come when he 's ready."

This information was not very explicit, and in truth added little to the youths' stock of knowledge.

"You know," said Arthur to his cousin, "it seems a good deal longer when you are waiting than at other times. Logan can't be told from a Nippinock, even by daylight, unless by some one who knows him, and so he 's in no danger himself."

"It is strange that he takes so much trouble and runs so much risk for us, when I see no reason why he should."

"You must n't forget that he has always been very friendly to both our families, and you can depend on him every time to take the part of white people against his own race, because the white people have used him right."

"And he'll do the same as long as they are fair toward him, but not an hour longer."

"That's what Kit Gist said, and he added, too, that by and by some party of our people would commit an outrage against Logan that would make him their enemy and he would show himself worse than a thousand wildcats."

"Well," said Stanton, "that is n't likely to happen until we get out of this scrape, which I think is the worst of our lives."

Aunt Cynthia, having completed her household work for the time, seated herself on the opposite side of the room in the rocking-chair, which her brother had made expressly for her. She folded her hands and swayed gently back and forth, as if in deep thought, but her nephews did not fail to note one grim fact: she placed herself out of range of the windows. The boys did so from the first.

The candle which helped to light the room sat on the table. The fire had sunk considerably and needed replenishing. Stanton started to throw on more wood, when his aunt forbade. The weather was not cold enough to make the fire necessary for comfort, and the fuel was likely to be needed for other purposes.

Suddenly the boys heard a slight noise on the outside.

"It 's Logan," whispered Stanton, rising and placing his hand on the latch.

"Wait a minute before you open the door."

Almost immediately there sounded a gentle tapping. Stanton lifted the latch, but first cautiously peeped out. He saw that it was the Mingo, drew back the door, and the Indian stepped across the threshold.

As he did so, his amazed friends observed that he carried the brimming pail of water in his left hand, while his right was closed around the barrel of his own rifle and of another. Setting down the utensil, he handed the strange weapon to Arthur Oakland, with the words:

"Logan gives the present to his son."

CHAPTER XV

SPEAKING WITH A DOUBLE TONGUE

IT has already been made plain why Logan the Mingo refused to allow Stanton Bothwell to visit the spring near the mountain cabin. The distance was no more than a hundred yards, yet thus early in the drama did he deem it too dangerous for either of the youths to trust himself in the shadow of the gloomy forest. Although the Indian favored the immediate departure of the whole party, he would not have permitted it until satisfied that the start could be made in comparative safety.

The spring was on the margin of the clearing, just within the edge of the wood. The additional moisture thus given to the soil caused the grass to grow luxuriantly until late in the season, and it was easy for Winslow Bothwell to store up enough hay and cornstalks or fodder for the cow throughout the winters, which were sometimes very severe in that region. A shed of logs and branches was provided for the animal during bad weather.

As the Mingo stepped softly out of the door of the cabin, the faintest ribbon of shadow veiled his figure. This shadow would gradually increase as the moon passed farther over in the heavens until it extended several rods from the building. Beyond this space, in every direction, the flood of moonlight lit up the clearing almost as plainly as if the sun were shining.

Instead of following the path which led to the spring, Logan stood for several minutes so close to the door just closed behind him that his form was invisible to any one in the surrounding wood. Standing thus, he called all his wonderful powers of seeing and hearing into play to ascertain whether the dreaded danger was at hand or still at a distance.

The round moon had climbed far up the cloudless sky, and the surrounding forest was like a sea of darkness which rolled around the silvery island formed by the clearing. A deep, hollow murmur, like that of the far-away ocean, stole through the night, as if it were the voice of silence itself. No sound of rifle-shot or Indian war-whoop intruded upon the solemn stillness, though he knew that fierce wild men were hurrying like phantoms through the solitude, eager for the lives of others, and hungering for the opportunity to use rifle, tomahawk, knife, and torch.

But the interest of the Mingo just then centred in his immediate surroundings. His keen eyes roamed along every visible portion of the clearing, and it may be said that his hearing was trained to that marvellous point that it would have detected the falling of a leaf near him.

He neither saw nor heard anything to cause misgiving, and yet such cause might exist. Stepping off the broad slab that served for a porch, he glided along the side of the structure until at one corner, when, with a peculiar, loping gate, he trotted toward the edge of the clearing that was opposite the spring.

There was no special danger in this action and he was not alarmed. It will be remembered that he looked precisely like a Nippinock in his war-paint, even with his pail, and if seen by any of those bucks skulking in the vicinity was likely to be taken for one of them.

He did not increase or diminish his pace until he abruptly halted in the margin of the wood, when he spent several minutes using ears and eyes for all they were worth, and the fact that still nothing revealed itself was good reason for believing no enemy was near.

Logan's next proceeding was to skirt the clearing until he finally came round to the spring and the shed near it. The cow lay outside, contentedly chewing her cud, as her drowsiness gradually grew upon her. Being one of the stupidest creatures in all creation, she paid no attention to the shadowy figure that suddenly assumed form at her side.

Her indifference was another reason for believing that thus far all was well, and Logan did not hesitate to dip his pail into the cold, crystalline water and fill it to the brim. He was on the point of taking the direct path to the cabin, when like a flash he bounded to one side and screened himself behind the nearest tree. A soft, almost inaudible sound warned him that some one was approaching the spot.

It was a critical moment, and the Mingo smiled at his own remissness; for, unsurpassable woodman that he was, he had committed the oversight of leaving the filled pail standing near the spring where it was certain to be seen by whoever was drawing near.

But what of it? Let the intruder be the most terrible warrior of the whole Nippinock tribe, still the Mingo "had the drop" on him.

Although the stranger was invisible, Logan easily noted every step until he came to the spring, where enough moonlight penetrated the branches to reveal him dimly to the watcher. Of course he was an Indian warrior, but it was impossible to learn his identity, though every probability pointed to his being a Nippinock.

He knelt down and bent his head over the water, and the gurgling sounds, with the noise such as is heard when a horse is drinking rapidly, made it evident that he was quite thirsty. His sigh of enjoyment was audible, as he raised his head and drew the back of his hand across his mouth. Then rising to his feet, he started to move away when his foot struck the unnoticed pail and knocked it over.

The Indian was surprised and looked down to learn the cause. It is probable that he would have proceeded to demolish the wooden utensil had not Logan stepped forward as that moment and addressed him.

"Who is my brother that comes in the darkness of the night to quench his thirst at the spring of the evil paleface?"

"I am Wa-wa-mato, the Nippinock; who is my brother?"

"Great Bear from the Delawares, whose hunting grounds are to the north."

"The Delawares and Nippinocks are brothers; the Nippinocks have gone upon the war-path."

"And the Delawares have dug up the hatchet and are making ready to do so; they will fight for their French brothers; how fight the Nippinocks?"

"With the Frenchmen; not an Englishman shall be left to tell that they have set foot upon the hunting grounds the Great Spirit gave to his red children."

It will be understood that we are giving a liberal

interpretation of the conversation between these two aborigines, and it will be noted further that in the way of prevarication both proved themselves entitled to rank as Caucasians.

"It does the heart of Great Bear good to hear his brother speak the words that are like music in his ears; but why is Wa-wa-mato alone, so far from the rest of his brave warriors?"

"They are not far off; they are hastening to the fort of the palefaces that they may slay them all and lay their homes in ashes, but a few have turned aside to visit this cabin of the palefaces; we shall soon destroy all that are in it, and then hasten to help our brothers at the settlement."

This was just what the Mingo had feared. While the main body was passing on to the attack of Warrenburg and Fort Dinwiddie, a smaller party had been detailed to destroy the Bothwell cabin and its inmates. The real danger, it must be noted, did not lie in the attack from this smaller party, for there was little doubt that it could be held off for several days, but it was in the fact that it was almost certain to be reinforced by the principal company after its assault upon the settlement.

The purpose that instantly shaped itself in the mind of the Mingo was to convince Wa-wa-mato that he and his friends had no chance of success in attacking the cabin, and that the true course for them was to make all haste to aid in the more important enterprise.

"My brother is brave and he is wise," said Logan, "but his eyes do not see all that has been shown to Great Bear; how many warriors will attack the house?"

The Nippinock, somewhat curiously, was vague on this point, though it was impossible to say whether it was because of ignorance or with deliberate intent, but as near as the Mingo could make out, Wa-wa-mato had eight companions somewhere in the vicinity.

"In the cabin yonder," added the Mingo, pointing in the direction of the clearing, "are the two young men, and their father and Logan; each has a gun and plenty of powder and ball, and they long for the coming of the Nippinocks."

This, it will be admitted, was "drawing a long bow," but had it been daylight and no paint on the face of Logan, not the trace of a blush would have been perceptible.

And why should the listener doubt the assertion? And yet he did, and undoubtedly the cause of his doubt was the overturned waterpail. He may not have been able clearly to understand the reason for its presence, but it is certain his suspicion was awakened.

The announcement that Logan had made common cause with the defenders of the cabin did not seem to surprise the Nippinock, though it caused some vigorous words on his part.

"Logan is a dog! he is a coward! he speaks with a double tongue, and his heart is white like the palefaces'! He is not a son of the Great Spirit."

That the Mingo could restrain his rage and dissemble when necessary was proven by the calmness with which he listened to this fiery denunciation. His fingers itched to grasp the throat of the warrior and bear him to the earth in the final struggle.

Suddenly Wa-wa-mato asked:

"Who whispered in the ear of my brother that Logan is in the cabin of the paleface?"

"Great Bear saw him and the paleface whose home is yonder pass through the door, when the moon had been but a short time in the sky."

"And why did not Great Bear shoot the dog of a Logan?"

"He had with him the paleface whose rifle never misses; the life of Logan was not worth that of Great Bear. Where is Lame Panther, the great chief of the Nippinocks?"

Wa-wa-mato started and peered intently through the gloom into the face of the one who asked this question.

"Woe is me! He has gone to his happy hunting grounds; while he was giving the hand of friendship to Logan and three of his people, they shot him. When he was dying on the ground he killed two of the dogs, and but for his wounds, he would have slain all four."

"It is a lie!" interrupted the Mingo in a burst of unrestrainable rage; "I am Logan!"

CHAPTER XVI

THE MINGO'S RETURN

DESPITE his overpowering anger, Logan the Mingo retained his mastery of the situation. Whatever the nature of the suspicion in the mind of the Nippinock, he was not aware of the identity of the terrible Mingo until he himself announced it. As the words escaped the lips of Logan, he whipped out his knife and confronted Wa-wa-mato.

Thus, by a species of rude chivalry, he gave his enemy warning and allowed him opportunity to defend himself; but the Nippinock was cowardly, or perhaps was overawed by the fearful personality of the Mingo. He held his rifle in his left hand, and he dropped his right to his sash, in which rested his tomahawk and knife, but he failed to draw either weapon.

Logan could not attack him so long as he maintained this attitude, and he now tried to rouse him to action by means of taunts.

"Is Logan a dog and a coward? Then, why does Wa-wa-mato stand dumb and fear to fight him? Wa-wa-mato is the dog; he trembles like the dog before his master."

This may have been true, but, if so, the Nippinock continued to tremble. He made no attempt to use any of his weapons, nor did he speak or so much as stir. Few Indians would have been disarmed by such meekness, but Logan was, and, filled with unutterable disgust, he said:

"The palefaces can use the rifle which Wa-wa-mato holds in his hand but dare not point at Logan, and Logan commands the dog of a Nippinock to drop his gun to the ground that Logan may pick it up."

Without any hesitation, the Nippinock allowed the larger weapon to fall from his grasp to the earth between them. No conquest could have been more utter.

Logan contemplated him with unspeakable scorn for a full minute, and then extending his arm commanded:

"Go, dog! a true warrior does not attack him who is afraid to fight!"

Wa-wa-mato, with sealed lips, turned to obey the command, which must have been a welcome one to him. Logan stepped forward to claim the trophy, when with the quickness of a panther the Nippinock, who, unobserved in the gloom, had drawn his tomahawk, drew back his arm, whirled about, and hurled the missile with all the vicious energy of his nature, straight at the head of the Mingo.

As has been said, the latter was in the act of stooping to pick up the captured rifle, and his change of position helped him, but with inimitable dexterity he dropped his head still lower, and the weapon whizzed over his crown, missing it by scarcely an inch, striking the earth and turning end over end until it came to rest far to the rear.

Before the implement had ceased its gyrations, and before, therefore, the Nippinock comprehended his failure, the Mingo straightened up and his own tomahawk left his hand with a swiftness that no human eye could follow, speeding through the brief intervening space like the dart of the lightning stroke, and with the unerring accuracy of a rifleshot. So sudden, indeed, was the taking off of the Nippinock that the expression sometimes heard in these days could be applied to him, to the effect that he never knew what killed him, for the missile was driven with a force that was almost inconceivable, and a speed which gave the victim not a second's warning.

The action of the Mingo was characteristic. First recovering his own weapon, which had done its duty with awful completeness, he made the gleaming blade, with the assistance of the tiny stream that flowed from the spring, as spotless as before, after which he carefully restored it to its former place behind his girdle. All the time he acted as if unconscious of the presence of the frightful proof of his mastery in the handling of the weapon.

His next step was to refill the pail from the spring, and he did so with a care that showed he knew the value that was likely to attach to every drop. Then he picked up the captured rifle and examined it as well as he could in the gloom. As he suspected, it was an excellent weapon.

"It will make the heart of my son glad," grimly muttered the Mingo.

Despite, however, the extinguishment of the Nippinock, the result in a certain sense was a failure on the part of Logan. He had told the warrior a fabulous story about the defensive force of the cabin in the clearing, and there was reason to believe the Nippinock credited it. If, therefore, he had returned to his comrades near at hand, nothing was more likely than that they would have followed the advice offered, and, passing the cabin by, joined the main party in attacking Fort Dinwiddie and the settlement of Warrenburg. This would have averted the danger to the household, for a couple of days at least, a period sufficient for the Mingo to guide them to some secure retreat in the solitude, where they would be safe from discovery. Ultimately he could conduct them by a circuitous course to the settlement, there to remain until all danger departed from that portioh of the frontier.

These thoughts disturbed the Mingo, as with the two rifles held by one hand and the pail by the other he passed along the edge of the clearing to the point where he first entered the wood, and then advanced through the moonlight to the cabin, where, as has been shown, he made his presence known and was admitted.

Having set down the water and handed the captured rifle to Arthur Oakland, he made sure the latch-string was drawn in and the door locked.

The boys required no explanation to understand the means by which their dusky friend had obtained the weapon, but they did not ask any questions. Arthur walked to the table, where the candle was burning, and carefully examined the prize.

"It's heavier than mine," he said, lifting it up and down, or "hefting it," as the expression goes, "but I could n't ask for a better gun."

"It is very good," commented the Mingo; "it was taken from a paleface."

"Why, how can you know that, Logan?"

The question was warranted, for the patterns of the old-fashioned rifles, whether carried by white men or Indians, were the same, as was necessarily the case, since the latter obtained them from the former. By way of answer, the Mingo took the gun from the youth and pointed to the wooden stock, where had been rudely carved the letters "G. H." No colonial Indian, and few modern ones, ever had enough book education to do a thing of that sort. It was self-evident, therefore, that the letters were the initials of the white man who once owned the weapon.

Logan was wholly ignorant in that respect, and he listened to the cousins as they strove to recall the name of some acquaintance to whom the letters could apply, but they were able to think of none.

Aunt Cynthia was as curious as the boys. She stood among the group, listening to what was said and studying the gun with interest.

"If that once belonged to a white man it belongs to him still; how came it in your hands, Logan?"

"I took it from the Indian who killed the white man," calmly replied the Mingo, looking her in the face.

"The scandalous villain!" was her indignant exclamation; "I hope, Logan, you punished him as he deserved."

The even, white teeth of the Mingo gleamed through his war-paint and he replied in his low voice and indifferent manner:

"*I did!*"

Even Aunt Cynthia caught the meaning of these words and dropped that line of investigation.

"What do those notches mean that are cut on the lower part of the stock?" she asked, pointing to them; "there are, let me see,—one, two, three,—eight of them."

"I can answer that," replied Stanton; "'G. H.,' whoever he was, kept an account of the number of Indians he shot, by cutting a notch in the stock every time he winged one. It looks, therefore, as if he had laid eight low before one of his enemies picked him off."

"Then *he* was a scandalous villain, and was served right."

"That depends on how he came to shoot the red men," said Arthur, who could not help feeling that she had warrant for her severe words; for it is useless to deny that many of the frontiersmen who have been idealized as heroes, and figure as such in the annals of the times, were simply brutes, deserving of no more mercy than the red Indians whom they hunted down like rabid dogs. At times they killed in mere wantonness, and their crimes were responsible for scores of deaths of innocent persons, for when the dusky warriors retaliate they make no discrimination of persons.

It looked as if "G. H." belonged in this category, but since there can be no certainty of it, let us be charitable and give him the benefit of the doubt. *Requiescat in pace.*

Arthur having his own ball and ammunition, Logan did not disturb that of his victim Wa-wa-mato. The old-fashioned smooth-bore rifle was easily fitted with a bullet.

When a lull came in the conversation, Logan suddenly stooped over and with a gentle puff blew out the candle. This left the room in semi-darkness, for the reflection from the fire on the hearth diffused a yellow illumination which enabled the inmates to distinguish one another.

The cause for the Mingo's action was evident. Too much light within the apartment would help their enemies, who might be prowling around the edge of the clearing, to locate and pick them off. A shadowy form moving in front of the windows, even if exposed for only a moment, was sufficient for a watchful Nippinock to drive his fatal bullet through the panes.

This fact, already apparent, Logan impressed upon his friends. Then he stationed the boys at the other side of the cabin, where there were a number of goodly sized loopholes. These being pierced in all the walls, Aunt Cynthia assumed the rôle of a sentinel at the gable end of the house. The Mingo's station was near the door, but he did not confine himself to any particular spot, continually moving here and there, and peering out from all the sides in turn.

CHAPTER XVII

AS UNDER A FLAG OF TRUCE

AUNT CYNTHIA accepted all these preparations on the part of the Mingo as proof of her prudence in refusing to leave the cabin that evening on the perilous journey to the settlement. Surely, if there was so much need of precaution when they were all within the cabin, it would have been fatally perilous for them on the outside, and the most the party could do would have resulted in their walking directly into the trap set by the Nippinocks.

Such was the reasoning of the good woman, but she did not reason well. Logan's preparations were not against what threatened at that moment, but what might come within the next few hours— an interval sufficient for him to secure the safety of those now dependent upon him. The reconnoissance which he made directly after his encounter with the Nippinock satisfied him that the other members of the party were somewhere near awaiting the return of Wa-wa-mato, with the report of what he had discovered.

They would wait long enough to give the whites a good start. Logan knew this, and could not forget that the blotting out of Wa-wa-mato blotted out also the scheme he had formed for throwing the lesser party of Nippinocks into a panic. The half-hour or more succeeding the return of Logan with the water was the most favorable period of all for flight by his friends, for the coast was clear. None knew this better than he, but it did not affect his line of action. The woman had refused to depart before the morrow; he had consented thereto, and he was too proud to change, even though he believed it involved the question of life and death.

His intention was, as the night progressed, to divide the company into watches, but he meant to remain awake all the time. It was understood, of course, that the moment any one made a discovery, no matter how slight, it was to be reported to him.

It certainly was singular that Aunt Cynthia won this honor. Logan had crossed the room and was standing behind the boys at a rear loophole, when she took the place of the Mingo on the other side near the door. It was perhaps an hour after his return from the spring, and she had not been five minutes on post, when she exclaimed in an excited undertone:

"Come here, Logan! I see an Injin as sure as I live!"

As under a Flag of Truce 137

The warrior and both the youths hurried across the room. The former sternly ordered the cousins to return to their places. That which the woman saw might be a trick of the Nippinocks to draw the defenders away from the point where they intended to make a demonstration or attack.

"My gracious!" whispered Stanton, as he obeyed, "Logan can be as cross as blazes when he chooses."

"He has the right, for he is boss here."

Stepping to one of the narrow windows near the door, the Mingo drew the curtain aside and cautiously peeped out. One glance showed that Aunt Cynthia was not mistaken; for, on the edge of the clearing, in plain view, stood a single Nippinock warrior in an impressive attitude. Attired as has already been described, the stock of his rifle rested on the ground, and he grasped the barrel with one hand, his whole appearance suggesting a bronze statue, for the pose was the most effective that an artist could have chosen.

It was evident from the action of the Nippinock that his object was to attract the attention of the inmates of the cabin. As he stood in plain view and within easy range, nothing was easier than for the Mingo to pick him off by a single shot from the window, but it has been shown that Logan was governed by a species of chivalry rare among his race which prevented his taking an unfair advantage of a foe.

The Nippinock held his position a minute longer and then raised his free hand and waved it toward the cabin. Immediately, Logan drew up the sash and fluttered his hand in return, but it will be remembered that that side of the cabin was in shadow, and the other failed to see the signal to draw near. Neither of the red men spoke, and, turning his head, the Mingo said to Arthur:

"Come here and tell him to make known what is in his mind."

"Maybe he can't understand English," remarked the youth, as he took his place beside his dusky friend.

"Say to him, 'Come; I will not shoot.'"

The lad repeated the words loud enough to be heard across the intervening space. It was that for which the warrior was waiting, for he immediately advanced with a dignified and deliberate stride, until within a dozen paces of the door, when he halted and dropped the stock of his rifle to the ground, grasping the upright barrel near the muzzle and assuming the pose already described.

Even before he had done this, the Mingo, with a peculiar feeling, recognized him as Leaping Deer, the sub-chief and orator, who had stood beside him on the fallen tree when Logan uttered his defiance to the Nippinock war-party and dashed through the amazed warriors to the wood.

Under the whispered prompting of the Mingo the following conversation took place:

"What does my brother wish?"

"Paleface come out house—Nippinock no hurt."

"Why then should we come out?"

"Nippinock burn cabin—take scalp—kill boys—kill woman."

"Then we may as well stay here."

"Come out—won't hurt—stay dere—we burn."

"You can't scare us, Nippinock! We are not afraid of you; we are all well armed and there are enough of us to beat you off."

"Ugh! Two boys—one squaw! Ugh!" scornfully repeated the warrior.

"Tell him," whispered Logan, "that I am here, and your father, and we have two guns for each of us, and our hearts will be glad when his people attack us."

Arthur Oakland turned toward the Mingo and protested:

"I can't tell him *that!*"

"Why not tell him?" was the surprised inquiry.

"It is a falsehood; I will not tell a lie."

The disgusted Logan called Stanton across the room, and ordered him to repeat the declaration.

"Do you think I am fonder of telling lies than Art?" was the angry question of the youth. "I would n't do that to save our lives."

The Mingo was about to appeal to Aunt Cynthia, but was stopped by her remark:

"That's right, boys! Tell the truth and leave the rest to God."

The situation was delicate. The sudden stoppage of the conversation was likely to confirm the belief of Leaping Deer, and Arthur Oakland, understanding this, resorted to a compromise, if telling the strict truth can be considered a compromise.

"Logan is with us," he said through the window to the Nippinock.

Most likely the fact that the Mingo was mute during this interview gave Leaping Deer the impression he made manifest.

"Big lie—paleface tell big lie."

Before the lad could make suitable response, he heard the door softly open at his side. Logan glided through like a phantom, closing it behind him. The Nippinock was so near that, despite the shadow, he saw and recognized the terrible Mingo, who calmly addressed him in his own tongue.

"Leaping Deer says my son lies! Here is Logan!"

It was a startling shock to the Nippinock, who held Logan in personal fear, and he must have felt the peculiar peril of his position, since he had placed himself wholly in the power of the inmates of the cabin.

And yet therein lay his security, for he was virtually under a flag of truce, which would be respected not only by the whites, but by the Mingo, who followed many of their ways. Leaping Deer was so amazed that a full minute passed before he made answer.

"When the sun is hidden in the sky, the red man cannot see what is before him."

"But the moon gives him the light that shows Logan stands before him."

This assertion, from the nature of things, could not be disputed, and the Nippinock gave a beautiful example of "hedging."

"Logan speaks with a single tongue; Leaping Deer sees that which he sees; Leaping Deer comes to the palefaces as their brother; Logan is a paleface."

This might sound at first as if it were a reproach, but it was not meant as such and the Mingo understood it as a reminder that his visitor was acting for the time as a messenger and not as a combatant, a fact to which Logan could not close his eyes.

"Leaping Deer has his gun and his tomahawk and his knife; Logan has his gun and his tomahawk and his knife; the palefaces will not harm Leaping Deer; let him and Logan lay aside their guns and use only their tomahawks and knives."

The Nippinock was readier with his response than would have been expected.

"The heart of Leaping Deer would rejoice to do as Logan says, for Leaping Deer fears him not, but the brothers of Leaping Deer are in the wood and they await the reply he will bring them."

It will be admitted that this was a clever escape from a bad dilemma. The Mingo was chagrined, but for a man of his principles there was no help for it.

"And what message will Leaping Deer take to the Nippinocks?"

"That Logan and his white brother and the two whose years are few are in the cabin, and they fear not the Nippinocks."

This declaration, which the Mingo had wished the boys to make, did not deceive him. Leaping Deer in hedging overdid it, for the word which he was certain to carry back to his waiting comrades would be the true one, inasmuch as the Mingo would have demonstrated the truth of his boast had it been in his power to do so.

CHAPTER XVIII

A STARTLING VISITOR

"LET Leaping Deer bear the message to the Nippinocks; let them attack the cabin and not wait, for Logan and the palefaces grow weary."

"And when Leaping Deer has spoken to his brothers, then will he make haste to fight with Logan."

It would have been as well had these words remained unsaid, for they did not deceive the Mingo, who knew his antagonist would never fight him on equal terms, but would always be quick to seize a treacherous advantage.

"Why does Leaping Deer linger?" sneered Logan; "let him hasten to his dogs of brothers and come back to Logan, who will wait for him."

With military promptness, the Nippinock wheeled and walked back over his former route to the wood.

The impulse at such times, when one is exposed to a fire from the rear, is almost irresistible to break into a run, but if such was the feeling of the warrior, he did not yield to it, but maintained the same dignified stride, until he slipped into the gloom of the surrounding forest.

Of course all our friends in the cabin were listeners to the conversation, though not a word of it was intelligible. They saw the Nippinock turn and depart, and then awaited the entrance of the Mingo with his explanation.

But he came not. The minutes passed without bringing his gentle tap against the door, whose latch-string was still inside. Stanton stood with his hand on the latch ready to lift it and draw the door inward until he became impatient.

"What the mischief is the matter with him?" he whispered.

The position of the Mingo, while talking with Leaping Deer, was so close to the cabin that he could not be seen from either of the windows.

"Find out what has become of him," replied Arthur.

Stanton drew back the door a few inches and peeped out. Then he opened it still farther and thrust forth his head.

"He is n't in sight," he said in astonishment, as he again closed the door.

"He may be at the rear or one of the ends; take a look through the loopholes."

"There 's no need of that," called Aunt Cynthia, who had been silently passing round the room unnoticed by her nephews in their excitement; "he moved behind the house, and then broke into such a fast run for the wood that he got there before that scandalous villain passed out of sight."

"He's off on some business of his own," remarked Arthur, "and there's no saying when we shall see him again."

"Why did n't he tell us what he meant to do or at least bid us good-bye?" was the querulous query of Aunt Cynthia; "I did n't think Logan would forget his manners."

"He would have forgotten his sense, if he had done any such thing," growled Stanton, who was resentful because the present perilous situation was due to the obduracy of his aunt.

"Don't be so pert," she snapped; "I was n't talking to you."

"Then you must have been talking to me," said Arthur, "and my answer is the same as Stant's."

"You are just as impudent as he; no, and I was n't talking to *you*."

"Talking to yourself, eh? Well, there's no need of letting us hear you."

"If you don't want to hear me you need n't listen."

"We were n't listening."

"Hush! if you give me any more sass I'll box your ears."

The boys dropped the discussion and gave their whole attention to the work before them; Arthur remaining most of the time near the windows, while his cousin moved back and forth, peeping through the loopholes, which it will be remembered pierced each side of the cabin, with the exception of that containing the door and windows. Thus every part of the clearing was covered, though of necessity there were brief intervals when the scrutiny was withdrawn from some portions.

Aunt Cynthia seemed to feel that her work was finished for the time, for she removed her chair to one corner of the room, where she was beyond reach of any wandering bullets, and grimly rocked back and forth, feeling in no specially pleasant mood toward her nephews.

As yet not a shot had been fired within or outside the cabin, and the silence was like that which had brooded for ages over the primeval solitudes. The straining ear could catch that soft, almost inaudible murmur which has already been referred to as the voice of silence and recalls nothing so much as the faint moan of the far-away ocean.

Within the imperilled home, the stillness in a certain sense was equally impressive. All that was noted by the boys was the gentle creaking of one of the rockers of Aunt Cynthia's chair, as she gently swayed back and forth. The fire on the hearth had been allowed to smoulder until only the partial outlines of the angular woman and the chair were dimly

A Startling Visitor

reflected in the yellow firelight. The soft rustle of one of the embers falling apart was noticeable and the little spiral of flame fully lit up the room only to subside in a moment to its former obscurity.

"Hello! here's something!"

Stanton was at the rear of the cabin, as he uttered this exclamation. Arthur immediately left the front and hurried to his side. Aunt Cynthia continued rocking her chair, without increase or decrease of vigor.

"What is it?" asked Arthur.

"I saw something move, in the edge of the shadow, a little to the right, out yonder."

Both centred their attention on the point, and at the end of a minute or two a peculiar flickering was observed, which for a time neither was able to identify. That it had something to do with and was caused by their enemies, they could not doubt, and it was another proof that the whites were under surveillance and the time had passed for safe flight from the building.

Suddenly an Indian warrior stepped out of the shadow into the full glow of the moonlight, and stood as motionless as Leaping Deer when he waited to attract the attention of the inmates.

"I wonder if that's another messenger," whispered Arthur.

"I wish Logan was here to answer him."

"I can do as I did before, if he knows enough English to be understood."

"But you can't tell him Logan is here, and when he finds he is n't they may make their attack."

"What of it? Have n't we each got a rifle?—and he may be of more help out there in the woods than inside the house."

"And aunty may make some use of your broken gun," chuckled Stanton.

A ringing box on the ear checked the unseemly mirth of the youngster. The lady alluded to had risen from her chair and stood directly behind them. Both became as mute and meek as lambs.

"You simpletons!" she exclaimed; "can't you see who it is?"

At that instant, the Indian raised his hand and made a peculiar gesture, immediately stepping back into the shadow where he was invisible. There could be no doubt he was Logan the Mingo.

But what did he mean by his action? That his gesture was intended to convey some message to his friends could not be doubted, but, after discussion, the boys decided it was meant to apprise them that all was well and he was on the alert, though it was hard to think of his reason for such notice.

The cousins kept that portion of the wood under scrutiny for a little while, hoping their dusky friend would add a postcript to his message, but he did not, and Arthur returned to his former position, fearing that something might have escaped him during his absence.

So far, however, as he could judge, all was the same as before. He scanned everything in his field of vision, and was still peering when he became aware that the room behind him was filled with an unusual light. Turning his head to learn the cause, he saw Aunt Cynthia with a brand which she had taken from the fire, holding it close to her face and blowing it vigorously. She was standing by the table, with the candle in her other hand, so that it was evident she meant to relight it.

While looking in astonishment at her, the brand broke into a blaze, which she touched to the wick, replaced the candle on the table, flung the stick back into the fireplace, walked to her chair, sat down, and resumed her rocking without speaking a word; and in doing what she did, she builded better than she knew.

Neither of the boys protested. In the first place, they knew it was useless, and again the gloom and obscurity of the room had become oppressive. They were glad to have the additional light, and relieved that the responsibility for it rested upon their respected relative.

Now followed an hour that was trying to all three, for their nerves were keyed to a high pitch.

The boys changed posts now and then, and never relaxed their vigilance. Aunt Cynthia rocked a while, then peered through one of the loopholes, after which she resumed her swaying as before, not once uttering a syllable. And during all this period, neither eye nor ear discovered the slightest unusual thing.

But the imagination of each was active. The youths occasionally consulted together as to the meaning of the stillness and inaction, and, though they could not agree as to the details of their theories, they decided that it had a sinister meaning. There was a vague fear that when the danger did come, it would be like a cyclone and assail them from every side.

The cousins were each in his regular position, and Aunt Cynthia had returned to her rocking-chair, when Arthur Oakland was thrilled by a gentle tapping on the door.

"There's Logan!" he exclaimed delightedly, as he sprang forward, raised the latch, and drew the structure inward; "you don't know how glad we are to see you!"

The Indian stepped across the threshold while the youth was speaking, and, as he did so, Aunt Cynthia uttered a cry:

"*That isn't Logan!*"

CHAPTER XIX

OOROMOO

IT was true. The Indian who entered the cabin was not the Mingo, but a daring Nippinock, aflame with treacherous rage.

But for the relighted candle, he would not have been recognized until too late. Learning by some means hard to understand the habit of Logan, he imitated him with amazing audacity. He must have expected to be hailed when he presented himself, in which event he hardly could have escaped discovery.

Never were Arthur Oakland and Stanton Bothwell so completely outwitted and dumbfounded. They stood transfixed for the moment, even when their glance had told them the fearful truth.

But the raging warrior had come among them with the intention of tomahawking and slaying all three, and he would have done the same with the awful swiftness of the lightning stroke but for a single person, and that single person was—Aunt Cynthia Bothwell.

Wonderful as was her quickness in detecting the

cheat, it was not so wonderful as the celerity of her action in leaping to her feet, snatching up the broken rifle leaning near her, and levelling it at the frightful intruder.

"You scandalous villain! Behave yourself or I'll shoot!"

If the words were not clearly intelligible, there was no mistaking the meaning of the "sign language." Before the Nippinock could act, the woman got the drop on him, and he was not keen of vision enough to observe, as had the Mingo, that the weapon threatening him was as harmless as a stick of wood.

The example of the ready-minded woman was contagious. Her prompt action lifted the spell that had held the boys powerless, and they brought their guns to a level at the same instant.

"Don't shoot," commanded their aunt; "I'll do all the shooting that's needed."

"I don't think you'll do much, aunty," replied Arthur, quickly rallying from his depression.

"Keep your guns p'inted at him, and if he goes to jumping about and hitting at folks, shoot! But wait till I say when. Oh! the scandalous villain!"

The youths smiled. Since they had their prisoner covered, they were not likely to wait for orders, should quickness of action become necessary.

Meanwhile, as will be admitted, the position of

the warrior was anything but pleasant. Arrested at the very moment he was about to play the tiger, his heart must have been filled with gnawing chagrin over his discomfiture. His black eyes glanced hither and thither like those of a serpent, but strange would be that man who failed to "behave himself," knowing that instant death was the penalty for his first outbreak.

The intruder, in stature and general appearance, resembled the Mingo, so that, when all the circumstances are remembered, the mistake of the boys was natural. There was a certain dignity in his pose, as he stood with his right hand resting on the tomahawk in his girdle, and his left hanging loosely at his side, with his weight equally supported by his moccasins. He had no rifle with him, the tomahawk and knife being better suited for the dreadful work he had in mind.

Doubtless he could have drawn both weapons, leaped at his victims, and begun the massacre in the twinkling of an eye. Such an interval is brief enough, but not so brief as the travelling of two rifle bullets, starting at a point less than a dozen feet distant, and, therefore, we repeat, the Nippinock did nothing, but with a grim stoicism awaited his fate.

He had no warrant for expecting consideration, but he must have known that the palefaces held strange ideas of warfare and often showed mercy where nothing could induce an American Indian to grant it. The failure of any one of his captors to fire the instant the opportunity presented apprised him that he had fallen into the hands of those who fought under rules different from those that guided the red man when on the war-trail.

"I don't see any use of my keeping this heavy gun p'inted at him, when it tires my arms and you can shoot as well as me," remarked Aunt Cynthia, partly lowering the weapon and glancing from one boy to another.

"There's no need at all," said Arthur; "we'll keep an eye on him."

By this time the question had presented itself to the youths of what should be done with the Nippinock, now that he was their prisoner. It looked as if he was a species of white elephant on their hands. Being a prisoner they could not kill him, and in case of attack, he would prove an element of weakness, since it would take one of the boys to guard him.

The most natural remedy was to turn him loose, or hold him until the return of Logan, who would quickly cut the Gordian knot. To the cousins a scheme presented itself of making him a hostage, but there were so many difficulties in the way that, after a few minutes' discussion, the plan was abandoned.

At this puzzling juncture, it was Aunt Cynthia who came to the front. Without a particle of hesitation she walked up before the warrior and demanded:

"What 's your name?"

To the amazement of Arthur and Stanton, the Indian thus appealed to promptly answered:

"Ooromoo."

"Can you speak English?"

"Yes—speak like paleface; what you want?" was the astonishing reply, delivered in better accent than that of Leaping Deer. It was clear the prisoner had understood every word since his entrance into the cabin. Arthur and Stanton listened in open-mouthed wonderment.

"Why did you sneak in here as you did?"

"To kill you—to kill them," he frankly replied, indicating her nephews.

"Oh! you scandalous villain! Are n't you ashamed of yourself?"

To this demand, it was evident Ooromoo could not think of a suitable reply. He therefore held his peace, but the boys, who were closely watching the painted countenance, insisted that something suggesting a smile flickered around the mouth. If they were not mistaken, it was a strange fact, but nothing ever was able to change their belief.

For a minute or so, Aunt Cynthia could not find

words with which to express her indignation, and, before they came, Arthur Oakland interposed:

"Ooromoo, if we let you go, what will you do?"

"Kill all palefaces I can—kill *you!*—kill *him!*"

"You're the coolest demon I ever saw," replied the youth, who would have been glad of some pretext for setting the warrior free; "the best thing we can do is to hold you till Logan comes and let him attend to you."

"Logan, the dog! he is dead!" came the answer like a flash.

At first all three who heard the declaration were startled, but a moment's reflection left no doubt in the minds of the youths of its untruthfulness. The Mingo was not the one to be disposed of in the offhand manner that these words implied.

Aunt Cynthia stood for a moment speechless, and then she turned to her nephews.

"Do you believe that, boys?"

"There is n't a word of truth in it," replied Stanton; "Logan can't be killed as easy as that."

"I don't believe it either. What a scandalous villain you are! You begin by killing people, and you've ended up by lying. What next?"

"There's nothing worse than that, aunty," remarked Arthur.

"That's what I've always said; do you ever read your Bible, Ooromoo?"

This question was beyond the depth of the Nippinock, whose painted visage calmly looked down into the indignant countenance of the severely tried woman, and awaited her next onset.

"What do you think we ought to do with you?"

"Don't know—don't care ——."

And then Aunt Cynthia proved that she no longer doubted what she ought to do; for, taking a single step forward, she deliberately smote the warrior on the ear, with a force that sounded like the crack of a pistol!

"There! that's the way I cured my nephews of swearing! I guess you'll remember *that*."

Arthur and Stanton were aghast, for was the occurrence ever paralleled! As for Ooromoo himself, his conduct was no less astounding. He stood like a statue, never speaking or moving body or arms, but looking coolly into the face of the woman who had chastised him, and this time there was no mistake as to his smiling, for Aunt Cynthia herself saw it.

But who should read the meaning of that smile? It either meant a certain barbarous admiration of the temerity of this unarmed woman, who dared thus to smite an armed Indian warrior in his war-paint, or, what seemed more likely, it was an expression of infernal purpose, like that of Satan himself—a purpose that could bide its time in order to make the return blow wipe out the unpardonable outrage.

And fate had so ordered that the question was to be answered within the following twenty-four hours.

"Don't be too rough on him," interposed Arthur, recovering from the shock; "remember he has n't had the benefit of your training like Stant and me."

"Yes, aunty; begin more gently; he does n't know any better."

"*Everybody* knows better than to talk like him."

"I don't suppose it sounds bad to him, because it is n't in his own tongue."

"If you don't stop making excuses for him, Stanton, I 'll serve you the same way."

"I 've nothing more to say, except that I 'm getting tired of holding this gun pointed at him. It feels as if it weighed a hundred pounds."

"Don't forget that this strange rifle is a good deal heavier than yours," added Arthur, whose weapon was beginning to wabble.

"Whoever saw such simpletons? Why don't you rest 'em on the back of a chair? Seems to me I 'm the only one here who has any sense."

"I believe you are right, aunty," replied Arthur, who, like his cousin, adopted the simple artifice, to the immense relief of both.

It was at this juncture, when Aunt Cynthia was about to assert her authority in another direction, that a knocking was again heard on the door.

CHAPTER XX

AT THE THREE ROCKS

"THAT'S another of the scandalous villains!" exclaimed Aunt Cynthia, in more excitement than she had shown since the beginning of the siege; "I'll open the door."

"Be careful," warned Arthur, who saw a dangerous complication impending.

"Don't you worry about *me;* I know what I'm doing."

She moved past Ooromoo and laid her hand on the latch, but, before raising it, glanced around at her nephews, each of whom was kneeling with his rifle supported by the back of a chair.

"Arthur," she said, "keep your gun p'inted at Ooromoo, ready to shoot the minute he gets tired of behaving himself, and, Stanton, p'int yours so you can shoot the next villain if he goes to tearing round."

The lad made the slight shift of aim, saying as he did so:

"A good idea, but we don't want any more visitors."

The lady softly raised the latch, and opened the door no more than an inch. In the ribbon of shadow outside, and only a single pace away, she saw the form of an Indian warrior, whom at the first glance she recognized as Logan the Mingo.

"Come in," she said, drawing the door farther open; "la, sakes! I don't see what kept you away so long; we need you here."

As the Mingo entered, Ooromoo, without changing his pose, turned his head, so as to look him squarely in the face. That Logan was surprised was apparent to every one in the room, and had he not been thus affected, *they* would have been surprised.

The careful Aunt Cynthia relatched the door, and turning about, asked:

"Have you ever seen this Indian before?"

A striking incident followed. With no more than six feet separating them, the Mingo and the Nippinock looked straight into each other's eyes for a full minute. Logan had rested his hand on the knife in his girdle, and Ooromoo did the same, without the action affecting the fixity of either's gaze. Their eyes gleamed ominously, and with a peculiar hissing sound, the Mingo repeated, in a tone barely more than a whisper, the single word—

"*Ooromoo!*"

And the Nippinock replied in the same voice and with the same manner—

"*Logan!*"

This time the hand of each grasped his weapon, and there was a moment of horrifying expectancy on the part of the spectators that the hurricane fight to the death was going to take place then and there, but once more the general peacemaker interposed:

"I want you to understand," she said, raising her forefinger warningly, and speaking in her peremptory tones, "that this is *my* house, and I won't have any quarrelling here! You ought to be ashamed of yourselves!"

An experienced observer of the scene would have noted one or two facts that were not fully apparent to the actual spectators. Ooromoo and Logan were deadly enemies, and though the same could have been said of Leaping Deer and the Mingo, or indeed of him and any and all of the Nippinocks, yet there was this difference: Ooromoo was not in the least afraid of Logan.

He was a member of the war-party who were listening to the impassioned appeal of Leaping Deer, when the Mingo defied the whole company and dashed away; Ooromoo was foremost among his pursuers, and one of those who came upon the lifeless body of Lame Panther.

Every fierce yearning of his nature for revenge was fanned to a white heat, and it can be hardly doubted that his audacious entrance into the cabin was inspired mainly by the hope of meeting the Mingo.

And now they stood face to face and neither was afraid!

Logan, as the more civilized of the two, felt that the interior of the cabin with the female an enforced spectator was not the place to settle their quarrel. As for Ooromoo all times and all places were appropriate. But only a few minutes before, he had received a reminder that he could never forget of the dominancy of the woman of the household. With that strange, shadowy smile playing about the corners of his mouth, he loosed his hold upon his hunting-knife and allowed his hands to fall by his side. Logan did the same and said:

"Nippinock, there are three great rocks, side by side that look like brothers; they are off yonder [pointing to the rear of the cabin] and not far; will Ooromoo meet me there?"

"His heart is happy at the chance and his footsteps will hasten to meet the dog for whom he has long hunted."

"How soon will the Nippinock be at the rocks?"

"He will go straight thither from the cabin, if Logan will not keep him waiting."

"Ooromoo will first hunt out his friends that they may save him when Logan is about to tear his scalp from his head."

The charge of cowardice implied in these words was more intolerable than the one of treachery, for the latter is common to Indian nature, while the former is not universal; but Ooromoo was as "handy" with his tongue as the Mingo.

"Ooromoo might be afraid of a *man*, but he has no fear of a dog or a squaw; he knows the spot and he will go there with only the Great Spirit as his companion."

Here was the agreement in as positive terms as language could make it. The Mingo had challenged the Nippinock to meet him in mortal combat, and the latter had accepted the challenge with a promptness that left no doubt of his earnestness.

"If Ooromoo is *afraid* of Logan, he will not come to the three rocks," said the Mingo, with the sole purpose of incensing his enemy, who controlled his rage to the point of retorting:

"When Logan goes trembling to the rocks, he will find that Ooromoo has grown weary with waiting for him."

It was impossible to make a sharper thrust than this, and it "went home"; but the fashion of indulging in mutual taunts, so common among Indians, had accomplished its purpose, and it was only a waste of time to continue it.

"Go!" said the Mingo, pointing to the door, "and make all haste to the three rocks."

The Nippinock, without a word, lifted the latch and passed outside. The moment the door was closed, Logan strode across the floor to the rear and peered through one of the loopholes.

When several minutes passed without his catching sight of Ooromoo, he was filled with furious chagrin, believing the Nippinock had used the opportunity to rejoin his friends and secure his own safety; but while the watcher looked, he saw a shadowy figure stealing along the edge of the clearing, until he reached a point opposite the rear of the cabin, where he disappeared.

The natural explanation of this was that Ooromoo had purposely walked over a wrong course, so as to mislead any of his own people who might be watching, and then had guardedly worked his way round toward the appointed rendezvous. This looked as if the Nippinock meant everything he said, and the Mingo was convinced that such was the fact.

But the reader must have been struck by one peculiarity of the situation, which should be explained before going further. The Mingo had gone from and returned to the cabin several times when apparently it was under surveillance, and yet he was in no way disturbed by his enemies, who detested him beyond the power of words to express.

If it were possible for him thus to go and come,

why could not his companions do the same and thus pass from out the shadow of death?

Right there lay the whole thing in a nutshell. The play of the Nippinocks was to bring about this very thing. They did not mean that the Mingo should escape them, and they saw little likelihood of his doing so, as he passed back and forth, but they plotted to include the other three in his death. If they could be induced to come out from the shelter of the cabin, they would leave hope behind, but so long as they stayed within the building, it would not only be difficult to dislodge them, but the effort was likely to be prolonged and probably would cost them several lives.

Undoubtedly it was this view of the situation that restrained the Nippinocks from firing their guns during the early part of the evening, but the discovery of the body of Wa-wa-mato near the spring and the report brought back by Leaping Deer must have caused a doubt on the part of some of the war-party.

However, the Mingo's knowledge of Ooromoo's character satisfied him that no obstacle would be placed in the way of his meeting the daring warrior, and he explained the situation to his friends, telling them frankly why he was about to leave them so soon after his arrival, but expressing the hope that he would not be long away.

The three listened with intent interest, the boys glad to be relieved of their watch and ward over the Nippinock who had just left them.

"Logan," said their aunt, when the Mingo had finished, "I am worried about you."

He smiled as he answered:

"Logan has no fear."

"You don't understand me; you seem to have so much trouble I am afraid you are quarrelsome."

Logan smiled more broadly than before, and then said:

"It is the will of the Great Spirit"; and, perhaps seeking to escape the bore of further conversation with Aunt Cynthia, he raised the latch and passed out without another word, leaving his friends wondering and a trifle alarmed over the outcome of it all.

Instead of taking the same course as Ooromoo, he circled about the cabin and loped straight across the clearing toward the place appointed for the duel with his Nippinock enemy.

The distance was short, and in a few minutes he reached the place he had named, the three rocks. Confident of finding his adversary awaiting him, he drew his weapon and, abruptly halting, looked around for the well-known form.

But to his astonishment, he was nowhere to be seen. Leaning against one of the bowlders, Logan summoned his self-command and repressed a growing suspicion and impatience. At the end of a half-hour, however, all doubt vanished.

"Squaw! dog! serpent of a Nippinock! he has fled!" exclaimed the enraged Mingo, and yet, strange as it may seem, he did Ooromoo an injustice, for that warrior, as we have said, did not hold Logan in the slightest fear.

CHAPTER XXI

A STRANGE INTERVIEW

FROM what has already been related, the reader will understand that when Logan the Mingo left the cabin in the clearing (with the exception of his last departure), it was with the purpose of acquainting himself, so far as possible, with the real nature of the danger which threatened his friends.

It has already been shown that the main party of Nippinocks were pressing forward toward the settlement of Warrenburg with the intention of attacking that and in the hope of making the assault a surprise. While the Mingo was debating with himself as to whether he ought to make all haste over the mountains and through the forest to warn his friends of their danger, he providentially met Budd Goepel, one of the scouts attached to Fort Dinwiddie, as the blockhouse was called, who took the important task upon himself.

There was reasonable hope of his success, for his experience and skill ought to enable him to elude and outwit the Indians, but it promised to be a close race between him and the war-party; for the

A Strange Interview 169

Mingo having defiantly announced that he intended to warn the settlers of their peril, the Nippinocks would be forced to their best pace.

However, as has been shown, Warrenburg must of necessity be left to itself until Aunt Cynthia and her nephews were extricated from their dangerous situation.

Moreover, it has also been made clear that the war-party had detached a number of their bucks for the purpose of destroying the cabin and its inmates, and it was this group that engaged the attention of the matchless Mingo.

The result of Logan's manœuvering and scouting was the discovery that instead of five or six Nippinocks, as he had supposed, there were fully double that number skulking in the neighborhood of the clearing, engaged upon some pre-arranged scheme, whose precise nature he was unable for a time to fathom.

What the Mingo feared was that the smaller party were keeping the cabin under surveillance to prevent any of the inmates getting away until the return of the main body, whose numbers would enable them speedily to overwhelm the defenders, burn the building, and work their will with the insignificant garrison.

To sum up the situation the only possible escape for our friends lay in their leaving before the return of the war-party, and the problem of the Mingo was to discover a safe way of doing this—seemingly an unsolvable problem.

That he was not fired upon when he moved across the clearing did not deceive him. He could have been picked off on more than one occasion, but that would have warned the two youths in the cabin, who would have put up a sturdy fight,—a fight that possibly might be successful, since the Nippinocks, despite the impassioned appeal of Leaping Deer, felt that the attack upon Fort Dinwiddie might prove a failure, and a signal or message was liable to come at any hour for those left behind to hurry forward to reinforce the main party and assist it in the more important work. When it is remembered that Leaping Deer, Ooromoo, and their companions numbered almost a third of those who had hurried to the eastward to assail Warrenburg, it will be seen that the reinforcement was considerable, and the Nippinocks might readily believe it would prove the deciding factor in the greater affair.

It will be admitted that the Mingo had a most trying task on his hands, and one that would have filled almost any person with despair; but when we see him again, he had forgotten almost everything except his consuming wrath against Ooromoo, the Nippinock, because of his failure to keep his engagement with him.

A Strange Interview

Logan had waited for more than half an hour at the three rocks, when, certain that his adversary had "flunked," he moved away, infuriated and desperate. Profound stillness still reigned on every hand, and instead of returning to the cabin, he walked in the opposite direction, not with the intention of deserting his friends, but to give his ruffled feelings time in which to compose themselves and him a chance to regain his tranquillity.

He made his way slowly through a narrow, valley-like depression, where the growth of trees and vegetation was so scant that his form would have been easily visible to any one in the vicinity. As always, he was on the alert, even in his moments of tempestuous disgust, and it would have required a marvellously skilful Nippinock to gain any advantage over him.

When he had sauntered for a hundred yards or so, he paused and leaned against the trunk of a tree, whose upper portion had been splintered by a lightning bolt. He was now calmer, though still savage and revengeful.

He had stood for perhaps ten minutes, when the restless, piercing eyes, that were continually darting hither and thither, fell upon something which instantly held his attention and caused him to straighten up and look intently at it.

It was no more than fifty feet distant, so hidden

by the gloom that the few rays of moonlight gave only a faint suggestion of its outlines, which seemed to be those of a person, stretched at full length on his face.

The Mingo's first thought was that that which he saw was a fantastical formation of rock, stones, or a mound of earth, which in the obscurity brought to mind the body of a person; but, as he gazed, the resemblance increased, until he walked forward to investigate.

Before he reached the spot, he knew his first impression was correct. That which he saw was the form of a man, lying full length on his face, as if in a sound sleep.

But while approaching, the Mingo was sure the sleep was the one that knows no waking, and the next minute he saw that the figure was that of a white man. He recalled that Winslow Bothwell, the father of Stanton, and the owner of the cabin in the clearing, had left his home some hours before, and he feared the inanimate form was his, but, leaning over and turning the head so as to see the face and disfigured crown, he recognized it as that of Budd Goepel the scout.

The fact was ominous. He had set out in all haste to warn the settlement of Warrenburg of its danger, but was hardly started when through some mishap he was discovered by the Nippinock scouts.

LOGAN FINDS BUDD GOEPEL, THE SCOUT   Page 172

A Strange Interview 173

There could be no question that he put up a brave fight, for he was a brave man, but he proved to be another member of the innumerable army whose only epitaph is that they died at the post of duty.

The fact we repeat was ominous, and the Mingo read its full meaning. The settlement knew nothing of the shadowy band of warriors hurrying over mountain and through rocky forest and solitude to its destruction. Sleeping in imagined security, they were liable to be aroused at midnight by the war-whoop of the Indian, the crack of the rifle, and the whizz of the tomahawk. The blockhouse itself might be able to withstand the shock, but what of the families sleeping in their own cabins, who did not know of what was coming?

But on this occasion, there was no question of divided duty with the Mingo, for the Nippinock war-party was already so far on the road that the fleetest runner could not overtake and pass it. Indeed the warriors must be close to their destination, for they had been several hours hurrying thither, and the Mingo found himself bending his head and listening for the sounds of the faint, far-away reports of guns that would tell the battle was on and the massacre begun, but the oppressive silence remained unbroken.

The Mingo was still listening and thinking, when his sensitive ear caught the sound of a guarded foot-fall. The glance which he flashed toward the ridge to the eastward revealed the figure of an Indian warrior, passing up the slight elevation, the moonlight showing his face turned away from Logan; and that no thought of personal peril troubled him was proven by the fact that the Nippinock did not once look behind him nor to the right or left. His attention was fixed to the front, and the vigor of his action made it clear that he was impelled by some urgent matter.

Something familiar in his gait caught the attention of the Mingo. He bounded forward a couple of paces, and then waited until the other came into fuller view.

Yes; it was Ooromoo, the Nippinock!

The heart of Logan gave a flutter of delight as he hurried after the warrior who had run away from the challenge, which he eagerly accepted, and yet in running away did not do so because he held the Mingo in fear, though it cannot be denied that appearances were overwhelmingly against him.

Logan sped over the intervening space as if he were a greyhound. When nearly up with his man, he purposely made a slight noise which caused Ooromoo to look around. As he did so, the eyes of the two met and they recognized each other.

The Nippinock had his rifle with him, and consequently the two were similarly armed.

The American Indian possesses his own gifts in the way of taunt and ridicule, but naturally now and then situations arise in which he is unable to do them justice. It looked as if the present was one of them, so far as the Mingo was concerned, for, instead of breaking out in violent denunciation of his enemy, he gave utterance to a sarcasm that, in its way, was clever.

"Ooromoo has lost his path! The three rocks are behind him and not in front."

The Nippinock had faced about and laid his hand on his knife, but he did not draw it, and, as he looked at the Mingo, fairly quivering with desperately repressed fury, he quietly smiled, and replied in a matter-of-fact manner:

"Ooromoo will fight Logan, but he must do something else first."

That which followed will sound incredible to the reader; for, after a verbal sparring that lasted only a few minutes, the manner of the two became, if not friendly, respectful and chivalrous. All taunts and insults ceased, and they talked together with deep earnestness and without a sign of hostility.

And yet they were deadly enemies and it was understood between them that after a certain thing was accomplished, they would meet in deadly combat, and neither doubted the good faith of the other, for the Nippinock satisfactorily explained his failure to be at the three rocks, as he had agreed to be.

But until the certain thing took place, the Nippinock and Mingo were in a state of armed neutrality toward each other.

CHAPTER XXII

THE SIGNAL FIRE

THE remarkable interview between Logan and Ooromoo did not last longer than fifteen minutes. At its conclusion, the latter resumed his travelling eastward, going at a pace that showed he felt the need of haste. Indeed, where the nature of the ground permitted, he broke into the loping trot which his race can maintain for hours without fatigue.

The Mingo remained where they had parted, gazing as if he could follow the Nippinock long after he had faded from view. Then he turned about and made his way in the direction of the cabin, but did not go all the way thither. He was seeking elevated ground, and having attained it, hunted out the tallest tree within his field of vision. That found, he climbed it, passing in and out among the branches with the nimbleness of a monkey until in the very top, where he ensconced himself, after the manner of one who had gained the best point of observation.

Such undoubtedly was his object, for he could

not only see many miles of the mountainous wilderness stretching in the direction of the Atlantic, but the field of gloom to the westward extended well beyond the clearing in which stood the beleaguered cabin where his friends were in peril from the merciless Nippinocks.

The heart of the Mingo rose in his mouth, for at the second glance to the westward, he saw a great light, as if the dwelling-house was in flames. Then the dull report of a rifle sounded through the night.

The sight was so terrifying that even the stoical Mingo held his breath for a moment in awful suspense, and then came a sigh of immense relief, for he knew it was not the cabin that was ablaze.

That the interest of Logan lay to the eastward was shown by his almost continuous scrutiny of the country in that direction. The full moon rode high in the sky, which was without a cloud, the soft, fleecy light resting like a fairy veil on the world of gloom below. Again the report of a rifle came from behind him, but it caused little misgiving, since he was well convinced of the cause.

Suddenly, while peering into the night in front, he saw that for which he was waiting. A bright point gleamed to view like a star that had just struggled above the horizon. Brighter and brighter it glowed, until any one who saw it must have known it was meant for a signal.

A smile came to the face of the Mingo, for the hope that had led him to climb the tree and wait so long was gratified, and the distant light grew until the keen eyes noted the fluttering of the flame that had expanded in strength.

And there was still more. Some one drew a brand from the fire and circled it with a peculiar motion about his head. When it had been swung a half-dozen times to the right, it was reversed and circled as vigorously in the other direction. Thus the signalling went on until the series had been repeated almost a score of times, when the torch disappeared.

What was the meaning of this singular performance? The signal was clearly intended for some one, who was not the Mingo, for he kept his perch in the tree, where it was impossible for him to make reply.

When the telegraphing ceased, Logan scanned the gloom behind him and near at hand, meaning that the response should not escape him, but he discovered nothing of the nature he sought; yet, though it was a disappointment, it did not cause any lessening of hope on his part.

After another quarter of an hour, the same performance which has been described was repeated, but it displayed a peculiarity whose significance did not escape the watchful Mingo in the tree. Whoever the man was that was circling the torch, he had not completed more than three or four gyrations with it, when he abruptly stopped, and did no more.

The meaning of this was that an answer had been flashed to his signal, and his duty, therefore, was ended for the time. He telegraphed nothing further, and a close study of the fire itself showed that it was gradually decreasing in strength, as if he who kindled it saw its usefulness was over and had taken himself elsewhere. Such, the Mingo was convinced, was the fact.

Logan was puzzled that with all his keenness of vision, he could detect nothing of the reply to the signal. It must have been sent from some point near him, and yet that could not readily take place without its being observed by him. Having seen all that he anticipated, he now descended to the lowermost limbs and dropped lightly to the ground.

He had performed his duty and his next step was to turn his face toward the cabin where his friends were anxiously awaiting his coming. Advancing cautiously, he was quick to discover that footsteps were approaching from the opposite direction, and whisking behind the nearest protection, he counted the phantom-like figures as they filed past. There were ten of them, whereat the Mingo smiled again.

Meanwhile, our friends in the cabin found the passing minutes full of anxiety. The departure of Logan was so unexpected that no one knew when to look for his return, and as time wore on without bringing him, a distressing misgiving oppressed Aunt Cynthia as well as her nephews.

They knew he had gone to fight with Ooromoo, and there was not one of the three who did not feel instinctively that the Nippinock was an adversary much the superior of Leaping Deer. Wonderful as were the powers of the Mingo, he was not invincible. Sooner or later, he must meet his master, and it could not seem impossible that he had done so in the case of the warrior who gave no evidence of being afraid of him, even though he had meekly submitted to the insult of Aunt Cynthia, the most helpless member of the little company.

Although the hour was waxing late, there was no drowsiness within the cabin. Aunt Cynthia snuffed the candle, and returned to her rocking-chair in the corner, though disposed now and then to take part in the fragmentary conversation. Stanton oscillated along the three sides of the building, while Arthur gave his principal attention to the door and the two windows.

The waiting would have become intolerable, but for an unexpected interruption. While faithfully attending to his duty, the boy distinguished the glow of burning wood, just beyond the edge of the clearing, and excitedly made known the fact. His friends were at his side in an instant, peering through the narrow window, whose sash was still raised.

"They have set fire to the shed!" exclaimed Stanton.

"The scandalous villains!" added his aunt; "there does n't seem anything too wicked for them folks to do. But I 'm glad of one thing."

"What 's that?"

"The cow was n't in the shed, for the weather is n't quite cold enough."

"Don't you be too sure that *that* makes any difference," said Arthur.

"Won't it save her from being burned to death? Seems to me, Arthur, you 're getting less sense every day of your life."

Under the circumstances, the boy did not think it worth while to explain.

"I forgot that she camped outside."

"I wonder," said the aunt, as the thought flashed upon her, "whether them villains dare do anything to our cow."

"It would be just like them," replied Stanton, "but whatever they have done or may do can't be helped, and there 's no use of thinking about it."

"If I only knew they had harmed her——"

Aunt Cynthia's remark ended in a scream, as she leaped backward, and the boys were hardly less startled by the jingle of glass, seemingly in their very eyes. A rifle had been fired from the wood, and the bullet passed so close to all three that there was no doubt at whom it was fired. The wonder is that no one was injured, for they had done a reckless thing in thus exposing themselves to the aim of the Nippinocks.

"We 've had enough of that," remarked Stanton, stepping to the table and blowing out the candle; "I don't understand why they did n't shoot at us before."

The extinguishment of the light left the room in almost complete darkness, for only a few embers remained on the hearth. The night was well advanced, but no one spoke of sleep, for slumber for a long time was impossible with the danger so imminent.

Arthur Oakland was the coolest of the three. Carefully sheltering himself, he peeped around the side of the window, watching the flames of the shed, and on the alert for a chance to give the Nippinocks a return shot. The flimsy structure burned rapidly and the blaze soon began to subside. Nothing had been heard of the cow, and he was intently peering in that direction, when he saw a shadowy figure moving between him and the light. There could be no mistake as to its identity, and hast'ly aiming his gun, he let fly.

The howl of the warrior pierced the night, and he

leaped four or five feet in air, disappearing in the twinkling of an eye; but the mistake of Arthur was in being too quick, for, although unquestionably he had hit the hostile, he had only nipped him and left him as potent as ever for mischief. One good purpose, however, had been served: the red men became more chary about firing at the whites.

It looked as if the Nippinocks were growing impatient and had determined to begin offensive operations, but were now checked by the readiness and aim of the defenders.

None could have been more vigilant than our friends. Aunt Cynthia abandoned her rocking-chair, and helped Stanton in keeping watch from all three sides of the cabin. Arthur occasionally joined them, but a feeling that the real danger threatened from his side held him at his post for most of the time.

Now followed a long period of expectancy, and it was a mystery to the inmates that so long a time passed without their seeing or hearing any more of their enemies. The discovery when made was by Stanton, who called out:

"Yonder is an Indian, sneaking along the wood!"

"Why don't you shoot him?" called back his cousin, as he and Aunt Cynthia hurried to his side.

"I'm afraid it may be Logan," replied Stanton.

"And that's who it is," added the aunt the same moment. The Mingo was recognized by the happy boys, as he came across the clearing at a deliberate stride, and the door was opened for him before he reached it.

CHAPTER XXIII

A SLIP

THE full moon had passed beyond the meridian, and was still undimmed by the fleecy fragment of a cloud. From the farther edge of the clearing extended the broad band of shadow cast by the fringe of forest, and the same solemn stillness rested upon mountain, wood, and stream. Still, had one been stationed on the summit of the high ridge to the eastward, his straining ear would have been able to catch faint but ominous sounds.

From far away in the direction of Fort Dinwiddie came the throbbing and almost inaudible reports of rifles which, but for the absolute quiet in the atmosphere, would hardly have travelled half that distance. The Nippinock war-party had reached the settlement and were pressing their attack with ferocious energy, and who shall foretell the end?

It will be recalled that when our friends in the cabin received the startling warning of the danger to which the light of the candle exposed them, it was extinguished. The fire on the hearth was permitted to wholly die out, and the darkness and silence of the tomb brooded over and within the building.

But it would have required no very observant eye to detect signs of life along the edge of the wood. Shadowy forms were moving silently to and fro, occasionally meeting and exchanging a sentence or two, in order to prevent any misunderstanding as to the plan of campaign that evidently had been determined upon. Then they melted away from one another and resumed their ghostly surveillance of the cabin.

The American Indian, when necessary, has the patience of the Eskimo, who will wait for twenty hours beside an air-hole, spear in hand, without moving a muscle until the seal pokes his nose above the surface, but when the warrior sees no need of waiting, it irks him to do so.

Hours had passed since the little party of whites took refuge in the cabin. With them was the detested Logan, who had slain the great war-chief Lame Panther and the warrior Wa-wa-mato. Intense as was their hatred of all palefaces, the emotion was "calm as a babe's slumber," compared with the rage felt toward him. They had spared him to enter and leave the structure under the belief that a false sense of security would lead him to bring forth the whites, with the result that all would be entrapped, without exposing the Nippinocks to the danger involved in an open attack.

Gradually, however, the conviction had come to the besieging hostiles that the Mingo had penetrated their design, and would not step into the snare spread at his feet. He had outwitted them, and while they believed they were playing him, he had deftly turned the tables.

Another belief had crystallized in the minds of the red men besieging the cabin: the main party that had passed on to attack the settlement would probably find a large contract on their hands and meet with difficulty in "delivering the goods." They would be able to give the besiegers no help for many hours to come, and the prospect of remaining idle for that length of time was intolerable. Therefore the lesser party were stealthily circling the building in the effort to find the best way of bringing about the destruction of the inmates.

Now, when it is remembered that one of the Nippinocks had stood within a few paces of the cabin, while conversing with Arthur Oakland, that their most formidable warrior, Ooromoo, had actually entered it, and that all had studied it with the closest scrutiny, it need hardly be said that they were acquainted with all its means of defence.

It will be recalled that the lower floor contained but a single door, with a narrow window on either side, the other walls being pierced with loopholes, which permitted the inmates to fire toward any

A Slip

point of the compass. Consequently a rush across the moonlit space, no matter from what point, exposed the assailants to the deadly aim of the defenders, who would spare them not.

The red man is fond of strategy, and hates to fight in the open. Hence the hesitation of the Nippinocks in their assault upon the cabin.

Finally all the besiegers came together near the ashes and charred ruins of the small structure that had been burned earlier in the evening. This position gave them a view of the front of the dwelling, though it was in shadow, and the total extinguishment of all light made it seem that the inmates were peacefully slumbering, but none of the Nippinocks dreamed for a moment of the possibility of such a fact.

The problem, therefore, was the very simple one of how the defenders could be captured or slain, with the least risk to their enemies, for, the circumstances being as stated, a small party within the dwelling could view with complacency an attack by three or four times their number, so long as such attack was open, and none knew this better than the Nippinocks themselves.

Among the group that gathered near the burned structure, the two most prominent were our old acquaintances Leaping Deer and Ooromoo, and the latter was the leader, as was eminently fitting, because of his greater courage, experience, and skill, the fame of the other resting mainly upon his gifts as an orator.

I am sure that the reader is wondering why the hostiles did not resort long before to their favorite means—fire; for it has been shown that the wood of the cabin had been so seasoned that it was quite combustible. A few arrows, wrapped about with burning tow, and launched with the skill possessed by all Indians, would imbed themselves in the roof and soon turn the structure into a roaring furnace.

There was one reason why the Nippinocks had not resorted to this means previous to their assembling on the edge of the clearing: they had no bows and arrows nor tow in their possession. The expectation that such material might be needed in the attack on Warrenburg caused the larger party to take all they had with them. Consequently some other method of attack must be formulated.

Standing grim and moody among his warriors, Ooromoo asked them to give their opinion as to the best way of bringing about the overthrow of the Mingo and his white friends.

One suggestion was that Ooromoo himself, under the pretence of seeking an interview, should secure an entrance into the building, but he impatiently refused the proposition by reminding his companions that his entrance was really an accident, which could never occur again, especially since the Mingo was now inside.

Another idea was for the party to keep out of sight and wait until Logan ventured forth once more, as seemed to have become his habit. It would be easy to capture or slay him, and a rush upon the building, defended by only two boys, must speedily overwhelm them. At first, it looked as if there was wisdom in this plan, but its one discouraging feature was that its success depended wholly upon Logan again placing himself in their power. His craftiness had doubtless given him a true idea of the situation, and the improbability of his doing as was desired was such that Ooromoo ended the discussion by declaring it impossible.

Leaping Deer set out to improve the occasion by one of his impassioned appeals for a cyclonic rush, straight across the clearing, that would sweep everything before it, but Ooromoo broke in with the question whether the orator was ready to lead the charge. Thereupon, he postponed the conclusion of his address.

There being nothing feasible in the propositions submitted, Ooromoo announced *his* plan, which instantly commended itself to every one. It was to protect themselves by shields, easily procurable from the ruins of the burned structure. Several of the awkward slabs and half-destroyed logs were large enough to shield the body of a man. By twisting withes tightly around them, an Indian could readily gain the grip that would enable him to hold his shield firmly in position in front of his body. Its thickness made it impervious to rifle-shots, and he could advance clear to the cabin, under as secure protection as if behind the stone walls of a fort.

A truth was known to all: there were a number of points close to the building which the defenders were unable to reach with their fire. The thickness of the logs cut off the command of the loopholes at short range, and once a foe was near the cabin, he only needed to be prudent to keep beyond danger.

An examination of the material on hand, so far as it could be made in the darkness, showed there was sufficient to construct two effective suits of armor. These were finished with no little ingenuity, the encircling withes affording the necessary grip, as has already been explained.

The peculiar arrangements for attack having been completed, Ooromoo quietly made known that the reconnoisance would be made by him and Leaping Deer. The latter expressed his delight over the opportunity to strike a blow at the palefaces and the hated Logan, but, if he deceived others, he did not deceive the leader of the Nippinocks.

Two grotesque-looking objects emerged from the shadow of the wood and began cautiously making their way toward the cabin in the clearing. Slightly in advance was Ooromoo, with a single charred slab, which, curiously enough, did not give him any protection from the knees downward. Consequently, a bullet could be easily fired from the building which would badly wound and place him *hors de combat*, but the daring warrior was always indifferent to danger and none of his comrades were surprised at his action.

But it was otherwise with Leaping Deer, who had bound two shells of logs together, and carefully held them in front, so that the shield projected several inches above his scalp-lock and touched his moccasins as he shuffled along, as timidly as a child learning to walk.

Neither carried anything in the nature of fire, and both for convenience left their rifles behind, but Leaping Deer held under his arm a bundle of twigs and dry branches, which he intended to place against the building, where he was safe from any shot from within, and could start the conflagration at his leisure on his second trip, from the powder in the pan of his weapon. It looked, therefore, as if he were to make himself extremely useful.

A disaster, however, overtook the enterprise almost at its inception. The couple had advanced but a few rods beyond the wood, being in the moonlight all the time, when Leaping Deer's excessive caution caused him to trip and, despite the desperate exertion to save himself, he sprawled headlong, breaking the thong, sending the shield flying several paces from him, and placing himself in fair range of the defenders within the cabin.

With a howl of dismay, the discomfited warrior leaped to his feet, and seeing the impossibility of gathering up his shattered armor in time to serve him, he dashed for the wood at a speed that fully justified the title by which he was known among his people.

There must have been a vein of waggery, as peculiar as it was rare, in the make-up of Ooromoo, for he shook so much with silent laughter that he was obliged to stand still until he could regain mastery of himself. No shot was fired at Leaping Deer, who bounded among his comrades in a shiver of affright.

Meanwhile, Ooromoo resumed his advance, more rapidly and recklessly than before, as if the escape of his companion had given him undue confidence in his immunity. Could the warriors in the wood have been able to see clearly, they would have observed that whereas his lower limbs had been only partially protected from the first, he now shifted the slab so far to one side that his head and shoulders were in plain view of every one in the cabin. It looked as if he held the defenders in so much contempt that he challenged them to shoot.

His remarkable progress continued amid the tomb-like silence of the building until he paused within ten feet of the closed door, and still not the slightest demonstration came from within. Standing thus but a moment, he flung his shield to the ground, and turning his head, uttered a shout to the watching Nippinocks. The cry was so peremptory a command that with little hesitation the whole party started on a run across the clearing.

As the wondering bucks gathered around him, he pointed to the door, where, to their amazement, they saw the latch-string hanging out, as if inviting them to enter.

The inaction from within had already raised a suspicion of the truth. Striding forward, Ooromoo grasped the string, gave it a smart jerk, and shoved the door inward. Without hesitation, he bounded across the threshold, and his followers swarmed after him. The leader kicked the ashes aside on the hearth, and catching up a brand, whirled it so vigorously about his head that it broke into a flame which lit up the interior, making clear the fact already suspected that neither Arthur Oakland, Stanton Bothwell, Aunt Cynthia, nor Logan the Mingo was within the building.

CHAPTER XXIV

OUT INTO THE NIGHT

THE events just narrated, in view of those previously made known, are quite sure to strike the reader as unreasonable if not contradictory. I hasten, therefore, to say that the advance of the Nippinocks, under the lead of Ooromoo, upon the cabin took place just before daylight of the second day and some hours after incidents that remain to be described.

Ooromoo and his disappointed warriors remained but a brief while in the building. He himself, torch in hand, nimbly climbed the sloping ladder in one corner, and searched the two upper rooms. It took but a minute to ascertain that none whom he sought was there, and he came down with the announcement. Leaping Deer proposed that the building be set on fire, and reached for Ooromoo's torch with which to carry out the proposal, but the leader shook his head.

"Let the cabin stay as it is; when the palefaces see that it has not been harmed they will think we have gone away, and they may return. If they see the glow and smoke, they will keep away."

This theory, when carefully analyzed, must show some weak points, upon which it is not necessary to dwell, but the one who was master propounded it and led the chagrined procession back to the wood from which it had emerged a short time before. They were not yet through with the business, as will appear in due time.

It was several hours previous to this occurrence that Logan the Mingo presented himself at the door of the cabin, and was admitted to the company of his delighted friends.

The first inquiry was a characteristic one from Aunt Cynthia:

"Did you hurt Ooromoo?"

"He has not been harmed."

"Did he hurt *you*?"

"Do I look so?" asked the amused Mingo.

"It is so dark in here I can't see."

Logan moved to the hearth, picked up a brand, blew it into a tiny twist of flame, and relighted the candle.

"Be careful," said Arthur, "you will draw the fire of the Nippinocks."

But the painted face relaxed into a grim smile, as the Mingo stood erect between the candle and the window pane that was shattered a little while before.

Aunt Cynthia scrutinized him closely, and then said with a sigh of relief:

"You don't seem to be suffering much, but Injins are such queer critters that maybe you 've got two or three bullets through your heart, and bimeby will flop over like a snuffed candle. I hope now, Logan, you will stop quarrelling so much, for it is wicked."

Arthur's curiosity compelled him to ask the question:

"Did n't you see Ooromoo?"

"We met, we talked, we will fight some other time."

This but added to the mystery, and the boys looked for further explanation. Since, however, the Mingo did not choose to give it, they had to content themselves with awaiting his pleasure. It was plain, however, to all that Logan was in good spirits over something, and his friends could not fail to feel the contagion. He seated himself in a chair so directly in range with the window that the alarmed Arthur felt obliged to protest.

"We have had one shot, Logan, and you will bring another. You are in exact range."

The Mingo cast an indifferent glance at the fractured pane, which had caught his eye before he entered the cabin. He did not move, but shook his head.

"No Nippinock there; all are gone."

This astounding declaration almost took away the breath of his listeners.

"Do you mean," asked Stanton, "that they are on the other side of the clearing?"

"They are gone; now we will go."

"Are we to leave at once?"

The Mingo inclined his head.

"Then if they have gone, what's the use of *our* going?" demanded Aunt Cynthia in her sharpest tones.

"Bimeby they come back—then we can't stay."

"But, Logan, you can't be certain of that," persisted the woman.

"Logan is certain; get ready, for we shall go."

His manner was the opposite of what it was earlier in the evening. There was no smile on his painted countenance, for he had realized his error in yielding to the whim of Aunt Cynthia in the first place. His expression was stern and there could be no mistaking his earnestness.

"Well," said Arthur, "I don't see that we have anything to do to make ready. There's nothing here to take with us."

"There's a good many things that we can carry easy enough, if you two boys were not so lazy."

"We take nothing with us," replied the Mingo with the same asperity.

The woman turned angrily upon him, full of rebellion, but something in the face of the Mingo warned her that he was in a mood that would stand no trifling, and she checked the words on her tongue and asked:

"Where do you intend to go, Logan?"

"To the fort at Warrenburg."

"But you told us the larger party of Nippinocks had gone there, and it seems to me we shall be in more danger than if we stay here."

"We go after the Nippinocks leave."

"Are we not likely to meet them on the way?"

So long as Aunt Cynthia was reasonable and tractable, her dusky friend was willing to be indulgent. With his old smile, he asked a question which contained the answer she sought:

"Are there not different paths to the fort and does not Logan know them all?"

"Of course," joined in Arthur; "I shall feel that when we once get out of this house and safely into the woods with him, we shall have nothing more to fear."

The Mingo looked fixedly at the youth and shook his head.

"The greatest dangers are before us."

These words were spoken with a solemnity that impressed all. Logan the Mingo was not one to call up idle fears, and when he spoke of the perils they had yet to face, it was with a grave earnestness that could leave no doubt of his meaning. But it was a strange combination of circumstances that had opened the path for his friends to the sheltering shadows of the forest, and, as they viewed it, nothing yet to come could be more wonderful.

Logan was not throwing away the minutes, for he knew how long it was prudent to stay in the cabin; but, since there was no reason to wait, he rose to his feet to signify that the time had come to leave the building. The others imitated his action. Aunt Cynthia looked keenly around, and then walked to the cupboard in the corner, where she drew forth a single article and held it up.

"May I take this with me? I can carry it in my pocket."

It was a small thick volume, which, in accordance with the fashion of the times, had wooden covers, and was bound with a gilt clasp.

"It is her Bible," explained Stanton.

"Yes," replied the Mingo, and the woman, with a murmured "Thank you," carefully adjusted the precious book in the pocket of her dress, gathered a shawl about her shoulders, arranged her old-fashioned bonnet, and, calmly looking at the Mingo, said, "I'm ready."

The next moment, the three were outside the cabin. Logan thrust the string through the hole above the latch, blew out the candle, and then followed, closing the door behind him.

The course taken was around the end of the building and toward a point a considerable distance from the ruins of the burned shed. The wood was hardly reached when Aunt Cynthia abruptly halted.

"Logan, you must let me bring the cow! I can't leave her behind; I insist on it!"

To the surprise of the boys, the Mingo promptly assented, and all three stood awaiting the return of the woman, who almost ran diagonally across the clearing after her valued property.

She was gone but a few minutes, when she came back at a faster pace than before, and was boiling over with indignation.

"What do you think?" she gasped; "the poor cow's dead! Oh the scandalous villains!"

CHAPTER XXV

HOW THE WARNING REACHED FORT DINWIDDIE

I NEED hardly remind you that the incidents I am relating took place on the eve of the mighty struggle between England and France in America known as the French and Indian War. George Washington, the young Virginian, was on his way to the French commander Le Bœuf, far to the westward near Lake Erie, with the written protest of Governor Dinwiddie of Virginia against the intrusion of the Frenchmen upon the territory claimed by the Americans, or rather by England, since we were still colonies of that country. The refusal to heed this protest opened the tremendous conflict.

Now, a wrong impression has been given the reader if he looks upon the outbreak of the Nippinock Indians as directly inspired by French agents. In one sense they were guilty, but, in a larger sense, innocent of that occurrence. During the intercolonial wars preceding the final conflict, the nation that succeeded in winning the Indians to its support held an enormous advantage, and each strove to bring about that result, the success generally being on the part of the French.

Foreseeing the inevitable war ahead, the emissaries of the latter were active and did effective work. Captain Eugene Choteau was one of their most trusted officers, and, starting from Fort Michillimacinac (Mackinaw), he spent several months visiting the different tribes and counselling with their chiefs and leaders. His policy was to win their friendship for France, so as to have their assistance when the actual fighting began, but he urged that nothing should be done in the way of hostilities previous to that time. Nations, like individuals, are anxious to have their opponents strike the first blow, in order to place themselves in the right light before the world.

Naturally, in the course of his journeyings, Captain Choteau came to the Nippinocks, where he urged the same policy. He made them many presents and more promises and received their pledges of support. In fact, he received more than he wished, for they insisted upon taking the warpath at once. Lame Panther and Ooromoo and others had their grievance. There had been an affray between some of their warriors and a party of white men, in which it is impossible to tell who was to blame, but it is quite safe to say it was the white men. Be that as it may, blood was shed and the relations reached the breaking-point.

Captain Choteau was alarmed to find the Nippinocks irrestrainable. As in many Indian conspiracies, their impatience precipitated events. It is a pleasure to record of the French officer that he acted an honorable course. His call at the Bothwell cabin, where, mainly owing to the handicap of his imperfect knowledge of English, he received rough treatment at the hands of Aunt Cynthia, was really with the purpose of befriending the family. Perhaps had he been less gallant to the lady he might have succeeded.

Despite his discouraging experience, the Captain persevered in his good intentions. It was hard work to learn the definite plans of the two Nippinock war-parties, for the leaders were suspicious of him and his "civilized" methods of warfare, but he succeeded in finding out that one party was bound northward, and since he could ascertain nothing more specific, and was unable to checkmate it in any way, he turned his attention to the other. Finally, he picked up enough hints to lead him to suspect that its intention was to make a secret and sudden attack on the settlement of Warrenburg, which was defended by the blockhouse known as Fort Dinwiddie.

Pulling himself together after his abrupt departure

from the cabin in the clearing, he set out to travel the twenty miles to the settlement that he might give the people warning of their danger, but he had hardly started when the startling fact broke upon him that the war-party was in advance, and was certain to reach Warrenburg first. He was accustomed to the woods, was one of the finest swordsmen in the French army, was active, alert, and sinewy, but could not expect to compete with the dusky miscreants, who were born in the forest and had spent all their lives there.

Nevertheless, he essayed the hopeless task. He knew the right direction to follow, and good fortune for a time attended him. Unacquainted with the trails, however, he made his way to the stream which Arthur Oakland had ascended earlier in the day in his canoe, his intention being to follow its course to the eastward; but, as straight as an arrow from the bow, he went to where the craft rested, and, had he not abruptly checked himself, would have fallen over it. There it was, with the long ashen paddle lying lengthwise in the boat, and the captain's experience in the wilderness had made him an expert in handling canoes.

"How kind of heaven!" he exclaimed in his own language; "I was guided to this spot that I might make use of this boat! My heart is filled with gratitude."

He lost no time. The graceful craft was shoved out into the stream, he leaping lightly into it and catching up the paddle as it shot out from shore. In an instant he had adjusted himself and was handling the boat with the skill of an Indian warrior.

It will be remembered that he was now going down-stream, and that the current was very rapid, but it also contained numerous rocks and obstructions in that portion, and, after several narrow escapes from shipwreck, he was obliged to slacken his speed and give closer attention to his work.

But the course rapidly improved. The stream widened, the obstructions were fewer, and, though the current became less rapid, the speed of the canoe increased under the sweep of his skilful arms, and it sped forward, like the skimming of a swallow over the water. Not only was the officer going in a straight direction toward Fort Dinwiddie, but he was travelling faster than the war-party deeper in the forest and headed toward the same destination.

It might be wrong to say he could outspeed those fleet runners had they chosen to call into play their wonderful powers, but, although advancing rapidly, they were not doing their best, for the reason that there was no call to do so. The favorite time for Indian attack is late at night, or a short time before daybreak, when people are supposed to sleep the soundest. The Nippinocks could easily reach the settlement by midnight, and, after a careful reconnoissance, make their attack as seemed to them best. Captain Choteau began to believe that if all went well he would arrive nearly at the same time, but there was enough doubt in the matter to make him extremely anxious, and even such arrival would be too late.

Down the lonely stream sped the birchen canoe, with the officer seated in the middle swinging the paddle first upon the right and then upon the left. The gloomy woods that lined the shores, the frowning bluffs, the moonlit sky, and the solemn stillness brooding over all and broken only by the dip of the blade or the howl of the distant wolf or cry of some other wild animal in the depth of the solitude, made the scene impressive and weird to the last degree.

Accustomed as Captain Choteau was to the most striking scenes of the romantic American forests, he would have felt the spell of his surroundings and drank in the poetry of the time and place, but for his dominating anxiety over the fate of that settlement, whose people dreamed not of the peril that was stealing upon them like a thief in the night.

Recalling what has been stated in our opening pages, it will be remembered that the canoe could serve the cousins for only a part of the way between

How the Warning Reached the Fort

their homes, when they were visiting each other, the distance at the eastern extremity of the water route being some two miles from the settlement. Captain Choteau was a good enough woodman to keep the points of the compass in his mind when threading his way through the trackless wilderness, and the time came ere long when the change in the course of the stream showed he was decreasing only to a slight extent the interval between him and Fort Dinwiddie. Finally, a sweeping bend in the broadening stream proved that to continue onward would take him farther from his destination.

The Captain had turned the canoe toward the left bank, with the purpose of landing and pushing his journey on foot, when a man, armed and in the garb of a hunter, walked out from the wood and came down the slight, cleared space toward him, walking slowly and with his rifle ready for instant use. He peered sharply at the officer, as if he expected the coming of some one and was uncertain of this person's identity.

But the vivid moonlight had revealed to each that the other was a white man, and, therefore, there was no cause for enmity between them. Having given the canoe enough impetus to send its nose sliding up the shingle, Captain Choteau laid the dripping blade beside him, and bringing his hand to the front of his cap, made a military salute.

"*Bon jour!* I bids you good-evening, zar; I ees glad to meet you."

"Good-evening," replied the other, with some coolness and dignity; "who are you?"

The boat touched shore, that moment and leaping out the officer drew it a little farther up the bank, and then turned about, hat in hand, and bowed low.

"Captain Eugene Choteau of ze ——th; and may I ask whom I have ze honor of addressing?"

"My name is Bothwell, and I live some miles to the westward."

"Ah! I am delighted to meet you," exclaimed the officer, cordially shaking his hand; "I vos entertained most charmeengly by ze good ladee of ze house; she is a noble ladee—ze gem of her sex."

Winslow Bothwell was mystified.

"My home is a considerable distance from here; have you come from there this evening?"

"Yez; I left in a leetle hurry, and I have come fast in ze canoe."

"What is the cause of your hurry?"

"Ah, my freend, I have bad, very bad news to take to ze Fort Dinwiddie."

"What is it?"

"A war-party of ze Injans are making great hurry through ze woods to ze fort; I mooch fear zat zey will arrive too soon."

"You are certain about that, Captain Choteau?" asked the alarmed woodman.

"Ah! I am zo sartin zat my heart is sad; zey will do evil work, for zey fight not like Frenchmen and Eengleeshmen; zey spare not ze women and leetle children."

"This is important news indeed," said Bothwell, much agitated, "but the fort is not far off and I will make haste to warn the settlers, who know nothing of their danger."

"You make my heart light again, my noble freend, and you will hurry faster zan I can, for you know ze woods better."

"Yes; I'm off at once."

"But one moment——"

"No; there's not a second to spare," interrupted Bothwell, who gave no thought to his own family, as he turned, plunged into the wood, and sped like a deer toward Fort Dinwiddie.

CHAPTER XXVI

ALL READY AND WAITING

WINSLOW BOTHWELL, as has been stated, left his home in the clearing early in the forenoon, with the expectation of spending several days in hunting. It was the season for such sport, he was a skilful hunter, and the woods abounded with game. Sometimes he took Stanton with him and occasionally, as in the present instance, he went alone.

His course lay to the southward and all went well until noon, when he made a discovery which caused him considerable uneasiness. From an elevated station, he gained a view of the Nippinock village, which he had visited more than once, and which he would have visited again but for that which he saw.

The warriors were assembled in the broad clearing a little to the west of the village, where they were engaged with much zest in throwing the tomahawk, firing at targets, leaping, running, wrestling, and occasionally venting their exuberance of spirits in shouts and war-cries. Moreover, even at a distance, the astonished spectator observed that most of the bucks were in war-paint.

All Ready and Waiting 213

A less experienced frontiersman might have misinterpreted the sight, but Winslow Bothwell needed no one to tell him that the Nippinocks had decided to take the war-path, for he saw before him the unerring indications; but he made the mistake of believing they would not do so for several days. He failed to see the imminence of the peril which threatened his own family and the settlement of Warrenburg.

His hunting excursion, however, was at an end. Watching the scene a brief while longer, he decided to go to Fort Dinwiddie and make known what he had learned, and then (believing he had full time to do so) would take his sister and son to the blockhouse to remain until the flurry was over. As it was, he thought it quite likely that some of the scouts who were continually moving to and fro would be ahead of him in carrying the news to the garrison and settlers.

Had his location been favorable, he would have first visited his own home and taken his family with him, but it was night and the journey would be unpleasant to his sister; and, confident that no risk was incurred, he took the shorter route to the settlement, travelling at so leisurely a rate that the night was far advanced when the unexpected meeting with Captain Choteau occurred.

The woodman might have doubted the news, or

demanded more particulars, had not that which he witnessed confirmed the startling tidings. If the Nippinocks were advancing against the settlement, the warning could not be carried there a moment too soon; and if the whole Indian strength were thus engaged, his own family had nothing to fear until after the attack was over, by which time he could look after them.

Had he tarried to hear a few more words from the French officer, he probably would have changed his mind and rushed to the aid of those a portion of whose perils has been narrated.

It was a race between the single white man and the Nippinock war-party, but with the important condition that the latter did not know there was a race. They advanced rapidly, but there being no cause for special haste they allowed themselves to be outrun, and Bothwell reached the settlement a half-hour in advance of the red men and he was not a moment too soon.

Fort Dinwiddie at that time was in charge of the famous scout Captain Ned Hunter, often referred to in the legends of the Virginia frontier as one of the bravest and most resourceful of those who risked all to protect the settlements from Indians, and many of whom did valiant service, not only in the French and Indian War, but in the struggle for American independence twenty years later.

It was near midnight when the self-appointed messenger reached the settlement, which consisted of seven scattered dwellings and the strong blockhouse already named. The fort indeed had been erected a considerable while before any cabin was put up, but the fertility of the soil, the favorable location, and the protection afforded by the garrison drew a number of families thither, among them being James Oakland, the father of Arthur, and his brother-in-law, Winslow Bothwell, who, for reasons already given, removed to a point twenty miles away in the mountainous forest.

The understanding of course was that upon the appearance of danger all the families would seek refuge in the blockhouse, whose garrison would not have feared an attack by several hundred Indians; but the real peril of the situation I have been describing will be perceived.

The members of each of the seven families slept in their own homes, when all looked well. A strong force of Indians could steal up and, with the furious impetuosity they often displayed, break into the cabins and massacre such inmates as had become careless through long immunity, or, failing in that, would be able to set fire to most of the cabins, and from the protection of the adjoining wood pick off the terrified inmates as they ran for Fort Dinwiddie.

To guard against such a disaster, two sentinels

were always on duty, at night, not within the blockhouse itself, for there they would have been of little service, but among the cabins, where they passed back and forth in the gloom and shadow, listening and watching for the first appearance of danger, with a skill due to special aptitude and improved by long experience and training. Their province, it will be understood, was not to detect peril a minute or two before it burst upon them, but in time for the exposed settlers to reach the shelter of the blockhouse.

That the sentinels were not remiss was proven by the fact that Bothwell had not time to reach the nearest cabin, which happened to be that of his brother-in-law, when he was called by name. One of the men on guard recognized him before he himself was seen.

It was no time for dallying, and the messenger, with a few words, made known the startling news he brought. A powerful war-party of Nippinocks were hurrying toward the settlement and were liable to arrive at any moment.

"Quick, Bothwell! Don't lose a second, Jim!" said one of the sentinels, addressing the other two men.

Instantly the three scattered and began pounding the doors of the different cabins and shouting in voices that could be heard even in the woods:

THE INDIANS ARE COMING TO THE FORT.

Page 247

"The Indians are coming! To the fort! You have n't a second to lose!"

Each man paused in front of a house and hammered until a response from within made it certain the alarm was understood. Since the number was so few it did not take the three long to make the rounds.

The first household aroused was that of James Oakland, whose wife was the sister of Winslow Bothwell. There was little time for hurried explanations, and one of the sentinels dashed to the blockhouse, whose massive door was speedily drawn inward and the terrified procession began streaming through.

There was no attempt to carry furniture, and only a few smaller articles that were no hindrance were snatched up and borne away. Men were too anxious about their wives and children, and wives too concerned for their husbands and children to think of anything else. Most of them were only half-clad. Mothers, their faces pale with terror, hugged their little ones to their breasts, and clasped the hands of the larger ones as they ran to the refuge, whose door stood invitingly open until it was certain not a soul was left outside, when more than one heart welled up with thankfulness to heaven for their escape.

While the panic lasted, strong men from the

blockhouse helped to bring in the women and children. They were cool, grim, and determined, but every one held his rifle firmly grasped, momentarily expecting the war-whoop, the shots, and the rush, and none was more thankful than they when the last person was gathered in the fold.

All danger of massacre seemed to have vanished, and, though there was the fear that the exposed cabins would be burned, yet the conditions of defence were found better than Bothwell expected.

In the first place, Fort Dinwiddie was an unusually powerful structure. It was more than fifty feet square, and consisted of two stories, the upper projecting several feet over the latter on all sides, the overhang being pierced with numerous loopholes, to permit the garrison to fire down upon the heads of any assailants who approached the lower walls.

The upper story was divided into several apartments and roughly prepared to accommodate half a hundred women and children, which exceeded the whole number in Warrenburg. In one corner of the lower floor, which was the ground itself, a well had been dug, and yielded an unfailing supply of clear, pure water, a means of defence as indispensable in the long run as powder and ball; for not only did it quench the thirst of the beleaguered ones, but it afforded the means of fighting fire, the most dreaded of all foes.

No one exposed to the perils of the frontier could forget the fearful weapon that seemed always at the command of the merciless red men. Very rarely was it possible to construct a building of any material except wood, though, of course, stone was generally employed in the chimneys, and when the structure itself was of masonry, the roof must needs be of wood, which in time became so seasoned as to be highly combustible. Since it was impossible to prevent the Indians from launching their burning arrows against the roof, the best the defenders could do was to make sure that the readiest means of quenching the flames was always at their command—and that was water.

The slabs which composed the roof shelved so steeply that the most agile warrior could not sustain himself unsupported upon them. At the peak was the box-like lookout, also loopholed, and containing a barrel of water never allowed to become empty. In addition, there was a trap-door on either side, from which water could be dashed upon any twist of flame the moment it appeared, and that with but little exposure by the garrison. All this being borne in mind, it will be conceded that Captain Hunter's boast of Fort Dinwiddie's being fireproof was not without warrant.

It need hardly be added that a supply of food and the necessaries of life was always in store, so that, no matter how suddenly a hostile force appeared before the blockhouse, it could not be found unprepared for a siege or prolonged attack.

It will be understood, therefore, that when the garrison was awakened from slumber by the news that an Indian attack was imminent, the principal feeling was that of annoyance in which fear had little or no part.

Moreover, Captain Ned Hunter, within five minutes after the closing of the door, displayed his self-confidence in so startling a manner that he fairly took away the breath of the stoutest-hearted scouts, though they speedily expressed their enthusiasm over the astounding line of action which he had determined upon.

CHAPTER XXVII

DIAMOND CUT DIAMOND

THE famous scout, Captain Ned Hunter, was one of the most remarkable men connected with the later colonial history of Virginia. Could it have been possible for you to meet him, you would have thought at once of the descriptions and accounts you had read of Captain Myles Standish, the military hero of Plymouth Colony of Massachusetts, for in appearance, and in many respects, they strikingly resembled each other.

Hunter was no more than five feet in height, but possessed prodigious strength and activity. He wore a long, reddish beard, and never seemed to know the meaning of fear. In all the numerous perils through which he passed, it is not remembered of him that he ever faltered or quailed. His intrepidity, honesty, and woodcraft made him a leader among men where every one was a hero.

Thus far, you will observe that the parallelism between these champions was complete, but in one respect they were absolute opposites. I doubt whether all New England ever held a more peppery-tempered fellow than Captain Myles Standish. He was like gunpowder, which flashes up and explodes at the touch of the tiniest spark, and, as a consequence, he was often in hot water when he need n't have been.

You have read of one peculiarity of the doughty Englishman: any slur upon his short stature was a mortal insult. One day, a tall, powerful Indian, standing among his companions, sneered at the little man and said he was only a boy who did not know how to fight. Hardly were the words uttered, when Standish with one leap had him by the throat, bore him to the earth, and slew him before any one could interfere.

Now, Ned Hunter was fortunate in being perfect master of his temper. More than one of his acquaintances declared they had never seen him angry. In this they probably erred, for angered he must have been many times, but never once was he known to lose his superb poise and self-control. Even his cool-tempered companions sometimes found his deliberation very trying.

Captain Hunter was sleeping when the alarm came to Fort Dinwiddie. He was lying in one corner of the extensive lower floor, on a blanket, without having removed his clothing except his coonskin cap. In a twinkling he was on his feet and directing everything. Comprehending on the instant the situation, he personally removed the massive fastenings of the ponderous door, drew it inward, and coolly watched the inflowing stream of terrified women and children. Acquainted with the members of every family, he studied each face as it came to view in the moonlight, whether infant or adult, and knew when the last one was safe within the blockhouse.

Meanwhile, several lanterns and candles had been lit, some of which were held in the hands of grave, determined men, while others were suspended from the hooks and supports intended for them. Their yellow light brought into striking relief the bearded, resolute faces, the pale countenances of scared women, and frightened children who hardly understood the nature of the sudden danger and therefore magnified it tenfold. Some of the younger, awakened out of a sound sleep, and held in the arms of their mothers, were crying, and refused for a time to be comforted. Everybody seemed to be flurried to a greater or less extent except the little man who almost unconsciously directed each movement, and who, with wonderful quickness, brought order out of chaos.

His first command was that the non-combatants, or women and children, should go to the upper story, make themselves comfortable, and resume their sleep,—as if the last part of this order were possible! The scheme which he had in mind, as I have said, was a startling one, and its success depended upon prompt action, and yet he uttered no hint until the last woman and child had climbed the ladder leading to the upper floor.

"Boys," said he, as the hardy frontiersmen grouped around him and looked into the keen eyes of the yellow-bearded man who, they instinctively felt, had something important to say, "there's twenty-six of us,—do you know that?"

No one had thought of making an exact count, and all were willing to accept their leader's estimate, which was larger than any one suspected, and therefore the more gratifying. Of course the Captain referred to the number of men in the fort, all of whom were fully armed. In addition, the seven women, two half-grown daughters, and three large boys knew how to aim and shoot, should the emergency arise. Fort Dinwiddie, therefore, was in admirable shape to make a stout defence.

"Them Nippinocks," continued the Captain, in his deliberate manner, "haint any bus'ness to bother us; they've come to kill our women and children."

Inasmuch as every one already knew this, there was some curiosity as to why the Captain thought it necessary to state the axiom. Evidently, it was meant to lead up to something else that was of more importance.

"*Tharfore*," he added, "my idee is to teach 'em a lesson that they won't forget for the next two hundred years."

"A good scheme, if there 's any way of carrying it out."

It was Winslow Bothwell who spoke, and he felt as did the others. Every one was certain that an important project had been formulated by Captain Hunter; they knew the Nippinocks were due any moment, and the deliberation of their leader was exasperating.

"Of course there 's a way of carrying it out, and we 're going to do it."

"For heaven's sake, Captain, out with it!" exclaimed the elder Oakland, who was so nervous that he could not remain still; "the Indians are sure to be here very soon, and it will then be too late."

"I don't know about that," and then, realizing the value of the seconds, Captain Hunter explained his scheme.

"Twenty of us will slip out into the woods afore the Injins arrive; we 'll take the best positions we kin find; they won't think about anything of that sort, and when they start in to fire the buildings, we 'll pepper 'em. It 'll be high old fun, boys!"

The proposal, we repeat, was a desperate one, for it required a score of men to leave the protection of the fort, where the advantage was decisive, and meet more than double their number of Indians on their own battle-ground and fight them in accordance with the red men's chosen method. The risk involved in this proceeding was too apparent to need description.

But the proposition "struck fire," and was received with ardor.

"It won't do to wait another minute," added the impatient Bothwell; "it will work if we go at it *at once.*"

"The varmints must n't think of nothin' of the kind," added a grizzled scout, "ontil we open onto 'em like forty thunder-storms, and then we 'll make the fur fly."

Captain Hunter could not fail to know all this. He named the several men who were to stay behind and hold the door ready to admit them at any instant, should it become necessary to retreat. Then the leader passed out with his trusty followers at his heels.

Just on the outside, at a whispered command all halted. The Captain emitted a soft, tremulous whistle, like the call of a night-bird. The next second it was answered from a point in the wood on the left and also on the right.

This proved that under the provoking slowness of their leader, he was capable of energetic action. Unnoticed by those around him, he had sent two of the scouts into the wood to give notice of the coming of the Indians. The signals just heard in reply to his inquiry meant that none of the Nippinocks had yet appeared.

"Scatter, boys, and let me fire the first shot!"

This was all the direction given. Instantly the score of shadowy forms fell apart; and without any attempt at concealment, for they relied upon the notice just received, they ran between the different cabins to the further edge of the little settlement, and then across the open space to the shelter of the wood. There they took positions behind trees and a couple of bowlders, which served for three of the men.

It was necessary for the party to keep well together, otherwise during the confusion and in the darkness they were liable to injure one another.

In preparing thus to attack their enemies in the rear, nothing could have been drawn more exceedingly fine, for two or three of the scouts were still moving cautiously about, preparatory to settling into position, as may be said, when a second signal, slightly different from the first, pierced the stillness.

It was heard by every member of the group and rightly interpreted:

"*The Nippinocks have arrived!*"

CHAPTER XXVIII

A VAIN HUNT

IT takes a wonderfully skilful white man to outwit an American Indian in woodcraft, and yet Captain Ned Hunter and every one of his companions did it.

The twenty rangers were all in position and as still as death, when their keen ears detected a faint, almost inaudible rustling among the leaves, and several soft whispers directly behind them. Cautious and guarded as were the Nippinocks in their movements, they knew they were in no danger of detection from the blockhouse, and that was the only point from which, as they believed, discovery was to be feared.

Then one, two, and eight or ten shadowy forms were dimly outlined on the edge of the wood, for the Indians were now in front of the white men, and their figures showed against the clear moonlight beyond. Others joined them until half the band stood between our friends and the scattered cabins, and were in more or less distinct view.

The remainder were at the rear, and some actually

among the whites, several halting within arm's reach. The situation could not have been more delicate and critical.

Then from among the warriors two moved noiselessly forward. As they did so, they adroitly kept the nearest cabin between them and the fort, so as to prevent discovery by any members of the garrison.

The blockhouse loomed grim and shadowy in the moonlight, at the further end of the clearing. The yellow glow from within showed through the numerous loopholes, as if the structure were a vast crouching monster, whose hundred unwinking eyes were awaiting the moment when its victims should come within its resistless reach.

Each of the two warriors, as he skulked forward without his rifle, carried a bundle of dried twigs, leaves, and branches in his arms. Their purpose was self-apparent.

The side of the cabin where one of the miscreants knelt was in the moonlight, and, being away from the blockhouse, was in plain view of the white men in the wood. Since the Indian was plying his deviltry against the home of James Oakland, and under the belief that all the family were asleep and were doomed to a frightful death, it cannot be supposed that the owner felt very graciously toward him.

"Why the mischief does n't Cap shoot?" was the impatient thought of Oakland; "I 'm not going to stand idle until the fire begins. Something must be done pretty quick!"

Suddenly two others sneaked forward, followed by three more, so that there was one for each cabin. The Nippinocks must have thought the garrison and the sentinels were unusually lax that night. If so, they soon changed their opinion.

The Indians had learned long before the use of the flint and steel from the whites, and that was the method they intended to employ in destroying the different buildings. Despite their extreme caution of movement, several were descried from the blockhouse, but, following the instructions of their leader, no shot was fired by the garrison.

Suddenly the stillness was broken by the sharp crack of a rifle, and the warrior who was stooping beside the home of James Oakland, making ready to ignite his bundle of fagots, uttered a single rasping screech, leaped several feet in the air, fell forward on his face, and never stirred again. It was Captain Hunter who fired the shot which let loose those of his eager companions.

A singular result followed. It being impossible to make any agreement upon the ones that were to serve as targets, the ten men who discharged their rifles almost simultaneously, wasted some of their shots through two or three selecting the same warrior. The consequences to these favored ones need not be named, but it was no more decisive than where one bullet sped true to its aim.

In an instant the edge of the wood became the field of the most terrific hand-to-hand combat conceivable. The scouts, who had given no attention to the prowlers among the cabins, opened fire on such Nippinocks as could be discerned, and then with shouts assailed them with their smaller weapons. The astounded warriors could form no idea of the number of those who attacked them with so much fury in the rear, and naturally believed their number to be double what it actually was. They scattered in a wild panic, but several fought so viciously that when, a short time later, Captain Hunter and his friends hurried into the blockhouse, they carried two badly wounded men, while the same number had been slightly hurt.

But the attack of the Nippinocks was a disastrous failure. Counting upon surprising the settlers, they in turn were completely surprised and overthrown with great loss. It was the timely warning of Winslow Bothwell that enabled Captain Hunter to perform the most brilliant exploit in the history of Fort Dinwiddie.

Not an adult closed his eyes that night within the blockhouse. Most of the children were soothed into slumber again, but none of the mothers rested until the sun was in the sky. Among those who came down the ladder to learn the result of the foray was Mrs. Oakland, who, as soon as the confusion permitted, drew her husband and relative aside to decide what should be done concerning a matter that weighed heavily upon all three.

Meanwhile, a sharp lookout was kept for the return of the Nippinocks, who had the inspiration of revenge—the most powerful of all motives—to nerve them to their worst. That a number of them were skulking in the vicinity could not be doubted, but they were not able to do any harm, and no doubt the main body had gone, taking their dead and wounded with them.

"Winslow," said Mrs. Oakland, "have you forgotten about Arthur and Stanton and Cynthia?"

"They have not been out of my mind for one minute, since I learned from that French officer that the Nippinocks were marching against the settlement."

"What do you think about it?"

"My home, as you know, lies so far out of the route between the Indian villages and Fort Dinwiddie that I am sure the band did not turn aside to molest it."

"But what about *their going back?*"

Bothwell swallowed the lump in his throat and fidgeted.

"I don't know—God protect them!"

"What I hope," said Oakland, "is that the boys and Cynthia have learned in some way of the coming trouble and have left the house before the Indians could reach it."

"Where would they go?" asked the mother, whose torturing fears made her keenly alert and penetrating.

"Naturally they would come here, Mary."

"Then they must be on the road this very minute."

"But," interposed Bothwell, vainly trying to fan the hope he could not feel himself, "have I not reminded you that our house is off the route to the Indian villages?"

"Not too far for them to turn aside and pay it a visit; if the main party does not do so, others will go thither, if they did not do it before coming here."

It will be seen that the sagacious woman was getting very close to the truth. Bothwell, as soon as he could command his choking voice, said:

"There's no mistake about Cynthia and the boys being in awful danger, and it looks as if we can do nothing to help them."

"At least we can *try*," said Oakland; "and we'll do it."

"I am with you," was the response; "for I could never remain here in uncertainty and suspense; *that* will be the trying lot of Mary."

"I shall follow you with my prayers," replied the mother, bravely repressing her emotions, as many a mother of the border learned to do under the most painful circumstances; "I am distressed and hopeful, but I know God will be with you and with the dear boys and Cynthia."

Having formed their resolution, the men delayed only long enough for a brief consultation with Captain Hunter. They bade the wife and sister an affectionate good-bye, and, drawing the Captain aside, acquainted him with their determination.

"I am glad to hear what you say, for it is your duty; do you want any of the boys to go with you?"

"What do you advise?"

"To take no one. If the whole party went, they would n't be enough to take care of the youngsters and their aunt in anything like fair fighting with the redskins. You understand, my friends, that there *must n't* be any fair fighting," added Captain Hunter significantly.

"It seems to me," remarked Oakland, "that the Nippinocks, in their rage over what has just taken place, will turn off from their regular course to destroy Bothwell's home and those that are in it."

"That is quite likely, but two other things may have taken place. Some one may have warned the boys and led them and their aunt to escape."

"Who would warn them?"

"Several of our scouts are out, and I have hope that that friendly Indian, Logan, may turn up in time to take a hand in the business. He would be worth a dozen of our best men."

It will be noted that the sagacious Captain also was treading extremely close to the truth.

"I never thought of him," replied Bothwell, "though I know he is somewhere in the neighborhood; he is very fond of the boys and they of him; but what other thing did you refer to as likely to have happened?"

"That Lame Panther sent a small party of his redskins to attack your house before the main body came here. It would be natural for him to feel more certain of surprising your folks than if he waited until his return."

Captain Hunter was without the means of knowing the fate that had overtaken the great Nippinock war-chief, but it will be seen that he had diagnosed the case with wonderful adroitness.

"But," he added, "all this is a guesswork and as likely to be wrong as right, so let it go; the thing for you to do is to get to the cabin as soon as you can."

"What route shall we follow?"

"Not the regular one, for you would be certain to run into the redskins, who will travel over the same. You must circle round to the right, for then, whether the varmints make for your home or for their own village, you'll miss them."

"If the boys would only do the same thing," sighed Bothwell, "there would be good ground for hope."

"Well, you can only 'trust in God and keep your powder dry'; I pin the most faith to that redskin, Logan, who, if he has not already mixed in this affair, is bound to do so pretty soon, and on the right side too."

The two men were on the point of moving away, when the deliberate Captain checked them for a moment.

"There's one thing that I don't understand,—and that is, that French officer who told you about the Nippinock war-party. What the mischief is he doing in this part of Virginia?"

"That is easy to answer; he is making a tour among the different Indian tribes to win them to the side of France in the war that is about to break out."

"Well, when the Nippinocks start in to hit us, he takes pains to send us warning."

"That is because they do not fight by civilized methods: he said as much to me."

"More likely it is because France is n't ready for the fighting to begin. Anyhow, he did us a mighty good turn, and I'll not forget it. Good-bye!"

Carefully reconnoitring the clearing and wood, to make sure they were not seen, the two men stole silently into the forest and started on their twenty-mile tramp to the cabin, about which we have had so much to tell. The suggestions of Captain Hunter were followed to the letter, their course bending so far around to the northward that they neither saw nor were seen by the vengeful Nippinocks. The route was a long and laborious one, which deprived them of the use of any trail or path, and taxed the endurance even of such toughened woodmen as they.

The forenoon was well advanced when they reached the clearing and saw the cabin unharmed and with the latch-string hanging out. Quite hopeful of finding their relatives safe and unharmed, they went forward, after some hesitation, and entered. Needless to say they discovered not a living soul besides themselves within the building, for the occupants had fled hours before.

CHAPTER XXIX

AN INSIDIOUS ADVERSARY

WE left Captain Choteau on the bank of the stream, down which he had hurriedly paddled in the birchen canoe, in the hope of reaching the settlement of Warrenburg in time to give the people warning of the approach of the Nippinock war-party, and the reader has learned that his humane task was successfully accomplished, with his help, by another.

But, for a while, the officer could not know how well he had builded. He would have detained Winslow Bothwell a few minutes longer, that he might tell him something about his family, but the woodman would not tarry, and perhaps it was well he did not, for the other had nothing to impart that would have been of help to the distressed father.

The mission of the Captain among the western tribes of Indians has been made clear. In every case, except with the Nippinocks, he received pledges not only of support to the French in the impending war, but an agreement that no move would be made by the red men until the actual outbreak of hostilities. A minor grievance precipitated the fight that has been described, with woful results to the aggressors.

The Captain remained standing in the cleared space, where he had stepped from the canoe, reflecting upon what had taken place, and what was certain to take place within the next few hours. He was something of a philosopher, and found comfort in the thought that he had done all that was possible for the settlers, and nothing more remained for him to do in that direction.

"This man will hurry through the woods with the speed of an Indian and much faster than I can travel," was his thought; "the distance is brief, and it will be idle for me to follow him; therefore I will not do so."

Then with a strength of mind peculiar to him he resolutely turned his thoughts away from Fort Dinwiddie to the cabin from which he had departed earlier in the evening. What could he do to befriend the lady and boys whom he believed still to be there?

You might suppose that because of the rough usage he received from Aunt Cynthia he would not feel well disposed toward her, but the opposite was the case. In the first place, his disposition and training made him chivalrous, especially toward the other sex, and then, though it may sound paradoxical, the rigorous rebuff she gave him deepened his respect for her. He could not help being gallant to all ladies, and his good looks and pleasing manner generally made such attentions acceptable. There was something refreshing, therefore, in meeting a rebuff from one of them, and he honored the woman who administered it.

However, it is not necessary to dwell upon this well-known quality of human nature. Suffice it to say that he was ready to risk his life to befriend the woman who he had every reason to believe was in sore need of help. He would gladly have done all in his power for the boys, but his chief concern was for her.

Now, it will be noted that Captain Choteau had no more actual knowledge of the situation of the party in the cabin than the parents of the boys. He knew at the time of his abrupt departure that the three were there, but was ignorant of Logan the Mingo, and, more important than all, did not suspect the visit that had been made by the smaller body of hostiles. His belief was that the whole Nippinock war-party, under the lead of Lame Panther, had pressed from their villages by the southward route to the attack upon Fort Dinwiddie, and that the real danger of the woman and her nephews would come upon the return of the body of Nippinocks.

It was this misconception of the actual situation

that threatened to bring all the services of the officer to naught, and which led him to adopt a line of action that was unique.

His belief was that the Nippinocks would suffer the frightful repulse which really occurred; that they would then start homeward, bearing their dead and badly wounded with them, and that Lame Panther and the unharmed ones would diverge from the route and turn aside to wreak their vengeance upon the dwellers in the Bothwell cabin.

Such being the theory of Captain Choteau, his course was clear. He must reach his imperilled friends as soon as possible, and apprise them of their danger. He ought to be able to do this before the hostiles could make the clearing, and the mountainous wilderness certainly offered hundreds of places where the fugitives could remain hidden until safe to press on to the settlement, or until an escort could be sent out to conduct them thither.

With these convictions in mind, the Captain once more shoved the canoe into the stream, and catching up the paddle began using it with all the vigor and skill he possessed, and that was considerable; but he was now compelled to work against the current, whose strength increased as he advanced, until in time the boat would cease to be of any use.

The officer had stood in meditation on the bank longer than he suspected, for he had not progressed far, when, with a start, he ceased paddling and listened. From the direction of the blockhouse came sounds through the solemn forest whose meaning could not be mistaken, for they were the faint reports of rifles mingled with the furious shouts of combatants.

A thrill of delight passed through him, for he rightly interpreted the sounds.

" 'T is well; Monsieur Bothwell has arrived in time; the settlers were prepared, and it makes my heart glad; ah, if it may be as well with the others!"

The outcries and reports lasted only a short time, but still the officer sat motionless and listening, and it grieves me to say that in a few minutes his head dropped forward on his breast and he sank into a deep slumber.

And yet he cannot be censured, for who can fight off the insidious approach of sleep? The strongest, most resolute man is helpless when "tired nature's sweet restorer" makes its demands. For forty-eight hours Captain Choteau had not slept for more than a few minutes at a time; he had walked far and labored hard with the paddle, and the wonder was that he was able to hold out so long, but he succumbed at last.

And as he slept the craft drifted, turning sideways with the current and floating so smoothly that it did not cause a ripple. All around was profound stillness and gloom, and boat and man were like the ghost of a canoe with its phantom occupant. Guided by that singular instinct which has saved us thousands of times from falling in our sleep, the officer placed the dripping oar in the boat beside him, folded his arms, and resumed a comfortable attitude, which he fancied would help him in doing some thinking that struck him just then as necessary.

Down the winding stream drifted the boat, until, a little way below where he had landed when he met Winslow Bothwell, the bow caught against the shallow shore and remained fast. The slight jar caused Captain Choteau to start and look around, but, observing nothing striking, he thought it his duty to do a little further thinking, and once more he sank into peaceful slumber.

His next awaking was of a character that kept him awake. It was a deep bass, "Ugh! my brother is tired!"

Fully aroused, Captain Choteau started up and stared around him. The canoe lay motionless against the bank, and around it on the shore stood fully twenty Nippinock warriors, all looking curiously at him. They were most of the party returning from Warrenburg to their village to the southward. Their dead and wounded were in charge of another division, which was pursuing its journey at a more leisurely pace.

After the death of Lame Panther at the hands of Logan the Mingo, the leadership went to Great Bear, who was a few years older than Ooromoo, though not his superior in courage or skill. He led the main party, while Ooromoo, as has been shown, remained behind with a squad to destroy the inmates of the Bothwell home.

It need not be said that the Nippinocks were in a vicious mood because of the result of the attack on the settlement, but the French officer felt no misgiving. He was well known to all these warriors, and, in truth, something in the nature of liking had sprung up between him and Great Bear. It was an intimation dropped by the latter, who had now become chief, that gave the officer the clue which enabled him to get word to Fort Dinwiddie in the nick of time.

The Nippinocks must have known that, despite their utmost caution, their advance had been discovered by the garrison. Such discovery they naturally credited to the vigilance of the white scouts. Could they but have known the truth, they would have made it exceedingly lively for Captain Choteau.

And, on the other hand, it is not improbable that Captain Choteau, at the same time, would have made it lively for his assailants, for let it not be forgotten that he still carried his favorite weapon and was the best swordsman in his regiment.

CHAPTER XXX

CHIEFTAIN AND CAPTAIN

GREAT BEAR, the Nippinock chieftain, spoke English better than Captain Choteau, who, however, was always able to make himself understood in the language of his hereditary enemies; but I am sure that in giving a part of the conversation between the two you will prefer that the meaning, rather than the broken sentences and faulty accent, should be recorded in intelligent language.

The whole truth flashed upon the Captain when he saw the sullen, vicious group, and his admirable self-possession remained with him. Rising to his feet, he stepped from the canoe, extended his hand to the chieftain, stretched his arms above his head, yawned, and replied:

"My brother, Great Bear, speaks the truth; I am sore weary, for until now it is long since I slept, and slumber overcame me."

"Where did my brother find the canoe that brought him hither?"

The quick-witted Frenchman saw he was under

some suspicion, and he skilfully steered clear of the trap set for him.

"I found the canoe on the shore, and I paddled down-stream until I closed my eyes with weariness."

"Where was my brother going?"

"To the settlement that is near at hand and has a fort."

"The English dwell there; they are the enemies of the French; why should my brother go there?"

"Great Bear has not forgotten the words I spoke to him; the English *will be* our enemies, but they are not so *now;* the time will soon come for the French and their brothers to strike them, but it is not yet. I would go to the settlement of the English, who know not their danger and would receive me as their friend; then I would study the fort and learn where it is weak, so that when the French and their brothers, the Nippinocks, strike, there would be no help for the English."

These words were as wormwood and gall to the chieftain. He had violated the counsel of his brother, and a woful disaster was the result. Captain Choteau knew from the fact that Great Bear was thus talking to him, that he was the leader of the Nippinocks, become so through the fall of Lame Panther, which naturally he attributed directly to the attack on the settlement.

Chieftain and Captain

Great Bear and his warriors stood silent and ugly. The officer had acquitted himself of all possible suspicion and he knew it. With something like desperate despair, the chieftain said:

"The words of my brother were wise, but Great Bear did not heed them; he and his warriors attacked the settlement, but some one had told the palefaces of our coming; they were ready, and there will be mourning in the lodges of the Nippinocks when our warriors return."

Captain Choteau threw up his hands in a well-counterfeited shock of grief:

"The words of Great Bear darken my soul! I am oppressed with sorrow; it is very bad, but, brothers," he added in a louder voice, addressing the group, "be not cast down! The French will soon come into this land; they will bring arms and powder and ball and many presents! They will join you in marching against the English, and when they return there will be none of them on your hunting grounds, which shall be given back to the red children of the Great Spirit! The brave Nippinocks that have fallen shall be avenged!"

There is nothing so sweet to the soul of the American Indian as the prospect of revenge; and, although the outburst of the officer was uttered in broken English, his manner did much to make his meaning clear to the few who knew nothing of the tongue. They swung their knives and tomahawks aloft and answered with frenzied shouts.

But the great object of Captain Choteau remained unaccomplished. He had done nothing to secure the safety of the occupants of the cabin in the clearing. Great Bear and his band were to the northward of the direct course to their villages, the one presumably taken by the party with the dead and wounded. This of itself was ominous.

Addressing the chieftain in a moderate tone, he added:

"Great Bear has said that my words were wise; then he will heed them and wait until the coming of his friends, the French, for many of them are now in this country and their armies are sailing across the deep water."

"Great Bear will do as his brother counsels; and he will not keep the Nippinocks waiting many moons."

"He has my pledge that we shall not make his heart weary with waiting."

But the officer was far from satisfied. The chieftain was not likely to look upon such an insignificant affair as the destruction of a single cabin and its occupants as a violation of his promise. Moreover, no reliance was to be placed upon the promise itself, for the word of the Nippinock was a broken reed. Whenever he saw a hope of success, he would attack with the fury of a cat o' mountain.

Had this band been further to the southward, Captain Choteau would have been hopeful. Perhaps it would change its course, but he determined not to be deceived by any Indian trickery.

"Where does my brother turn his face?" asked the dusky leader.

It had been in the officer's mind to remain with the band, but that would not do; for, if they pressed on to the cabin, as he believed was their purpose, he would have to stay with the party, witness the attack, and deprive himself of all power to aid his friends.

"He will go to the settlement, that he may see where the fort is weak, and come back and tell Great Bear."

"My brother does well," replied the chieftain, clearly gratified by the words; "Great Bear and his warriors will go to their villages that they may comfort those that mourn."

The night was so far advanced that signs of day were beginning to appear in the east when Captain Choteau bade the leader good-bye, and, plunging into the forest, set out in the direction of Fort Dinwiddie, but with no intention of going thither.

He did not look around until beyond sight of the hostiles. He had some misgiving that he would be followed, but saw no reason why any of the Nippinocks should shadow his movements, for what mattered it to them what he did?

When he halted in his tramp, he had penetrated an eighth of a mile into the trackless solitude, and attained an elevation that gave him an extended view of the country which he had just traversed. The sun was creeping up the horizon, and the increasing light revealed the winding stream over which he had paddled in the borrowed canoe, and many square miles of the forest on either side, though his vision did not reach to the cabin in the clearing, nor to the Nippinock village to the southward.

But the officer saw something which, above all others, he dreaded to see: glimpses of warriors, as they flitted in and out of sight, left no doubt that Great Bear and his band, instead of pushing southward toward their own lodges, were making direct for the cabin in the clearing!

I am sorry to say that when Captain Choteau saw this and understood what it meant, he uttered several exclamations, which it would never do to put in print. Omitting them, therefore, the substance of his addendum was:

"Why did the garrison spare *any* of the gang? Why did n't they clean out not only Lame Panther and a few of his warriors, but Great Bear and *all* the rest? It would have served them right, for they fight as savages and show no mercy to women and children. And now a score of them are making haste to revenge themselves upon one of the noblest of her sex and two boys! Infamous!"

And worse than all, eager as was the officer to aid the imperilled ones, he, as a military man, saw not one chance in a thousand of being able to assist them in the slightest degree. The Nippinocks were nearer to them than he and were proceeding in a direct line, though not making any special haste, since there was no call for it.

But Captain Choteau was not the man to remain idle at such a time, and the single fact that the Indians showed no hurry in their movements inspired him with the hope that possibly he could reach the clearing ahead of them.

There was no hesitation after he grasped the situation. He bounded through the wood at a reckless rate, tearing the underbrush, dashing around rocks, clambering over bowlders, sometimes running down declivities, leaping gullies and chasms, climbing steep slopes, veering to the right, then to the left, catching his feet in the running vines that were like metal wire, stumbling forward on his hands and knees, and immediately up and at it again, until he had placed several miles behind him, and, panting and exhausted, was forced to give himself a brief rest.

His situation was now such that he could not see fifty feet in any direction.

Precisely where the Indians were he had no means of knowing. When he listened, he heard only the panting of his breath and throbbing of his own heart; and, not waiting until fully recovered, he resumed his advance, carefully noting the position of the sun in the effort to avoid going astray in a solitude which made it necessary for one to keep his wits always about him.

It was still a goodly distance to the clearing, and he was obliged to moderate his pace, but he did not spare himself, and, when able, indulged in little bursts of speed that were quickly checked by unexpected obstructions.

One of the impossibilities at such times is to maintain a direct course through a forest unmarked by any trail. All of us know the singular tendency which a lost person shows to journey in a circle, and which is perhaps due to the unequal physical development of the right and left sides. The sun, too, as it climbed the sky, became a more unreliable index to the true direction. Finally, when the officer believed he had travelled so far that he was near the clearing, a vague suspicion came to him that he was astray.

He therefore took out his small pocket compass and examined it. The first glance he cast at the tiny, bobbing needle brought a howl of dismay. He was fully twenty degrees off the right course!

Chieftain and Captain

The Captain was in despair. It seemed as if fate had intervened to checkmate every move he made to befriend the imperilled ones, and, as he stood debating whether he should turn back or go on, he listened for the rifle-crack, the war-whoop, and the death-cry of the helpless prisoners; and that none of these sounds reached his ears was more than he could understand.

The divergence from the true route made it the more difficult to regain it, but a few minutes' hesitation determined him to press on, and summoning all his coolness to prevent a repetition of the blunder, despite the urgency of the matter, he did not move until assured upon the point.

"Ugh! brudder much run!"

Where he came from no one could guess, but there stood a Nippinock warrior, not ten feet distant, with his rifle, tomahawk, and knife, and staring wonderingly at him.

"Vat you vants?" savagely demanded the officer, laying his hand on his sword.

"Ugh! where brudder run, like deer?"

"None of your bus'ness—*Sacrebleu!*" and whipping out his weapon the angered Captain dashed for the Indian, who, with a gasp of affright, and forgetting his own weapons, bounded off with such speed that he quickly disappeared, leaving the Frenchman gnashing his teeth over his disappointment.

Again he took up his hurried advance, uncertain how much farther he had to travel, when, to his astonishment, ten minutes later, he reached the edge of the clearing opposite the burned shed. He was just in time to recoil and escape discovery by Great Bear and his band, who must have arrived some time earlier, for they were in the act of taking their departure over the trail on the farther side.

The heart of Captain Choteau was in his mouth, for, seeing that none of his friends were with them, he supposed all had been slain and their bodies were lying in the cabin. Hardly waiting until the Nippinocks were out of sight, he ran across the open space, tremblingly pulled the latch-string, and peered within.

And as he did so a great happiness came to him, for he knew (still ignorant of the smaller band of Ooromoo) that Aunt Cynthia and her nephews had fled before the coming of Great Bear and the main war-party.

CHAPTER XXXI

TRENDING TO THE NORTHWARD

INASMUCH as several parties have sought Aunt Cynthia and her nephews in vain, let us now take up the hunt.

Several curious coincidences occurred. Under the leadership of Logan the Mingo, the three left the cabin in the clearing shortly after midnight, when, for causes that will soon be made clear, the surveillance was removed for a time. A few hours later Ooromoo and Leaping Deer made their cautious advance, followed by the discovery that the occupants had fled in an unknown direction.

When the succeeding day was well along, the main band of Nippinocks under Great Bear reached the clearing, Captain Choteau appearing shortly after only to meet the same state of affairs. They departed, and the next arrivals were James Oakland and Winslow Bothwell, brothers-in-law, from whose hearts a great weight was lifted by the knowledge that their loved ones had gone, though naturally their anxiety could not be wholly removed until the safety of the fugitives was assured.

Now, in order to understand what follows, the reader must bear a number of facts in mind. Between Fort Dinwiddie and the clearing the distance was about twenty miles, through a rough, mountainous country, and the most direct route was that which the cousins always took, the main portion of which was by canoe.

The Nippinock village lay well to the southward of this route, so that a direct advance from it to the settlement would leave the cabin in the clearing well to the northward, while a deviation in that direction by any party would be noticeable.

When Oakland and Bothwell left Fort Dinwiddie they turned well to the right—that is, to the northward—in order to avoid the regular route to the Nippinock town, and the only other course they were likely to take, which was the short and more direct one. One of these was certain to be followed by the hostiles, and the action named, therefore, was a necessity.

Captain Choteau was obliged to do something of the same, and the probability is that but for his going astray he would have met the two men, and the meeting must have had an important bearing upon the events of the next few hours; but in such a wild and wooded section parties might pass within fifty or a hundred feet of each other without suspecting the fact, and the allies did not meet.

Going back to the time when Logan and his friends slipped out of the building and passed across the clearing, with the purpose of hurrying from the dangerous locality, it will be seen that the problem which confronted him, though difficult, was plain,— it being simply to get his companions safely to the blockhouse.

It need hardly be said that such a master of woodcraft as the Mingo could not make a mistake which our other friends were prudent enough to avoid. Instead of taking the regular route to the settlement, he, too, turned to the northward, but, in his case, his caution led him to go farther in that direction than the brothers-in-law, and, since his aim was to avoid all parties in the wilderness, it was not singular that he saw nothing of his friends who had taken the same general course.

Aunt Cynthia was in one of her most peppery moods. She had always acted kindly toward the Indians, and had given food to more than one Nippinock, and now they had compelled her to leave her home and flee for life. And, as if that were not enough, they had killed the cow, the only domestic animal owned by her brother!

"I wish I knowed the scandalous villain that did it!" she angrily added, after making known the incident.

"What good could it do you?" asked Stanton

with some impatience; "you couldn't punish him."

"But Logan could, and I'd make him do it!"

The Mingo showed no interest in these words, but checked further utterance by ordering no one to speak, unless in a whisper, and then only when necessary. The four had halted on the edge of the wood, where enough moonlight reached them to reveal one another indistinctly.

"Injin is there, there, there, there," said their dusky friend, indicating the different points of the compass; "Nippinock is everywhere; he hears the leaf fall, and when you speak your voices reach him, though he is a long way off."

This, no doubt, was an overstatement of facts, but it was safe to err in that direction, and the hearers were duly impressed, all being resolute to obey Logan in spirit and letter, for no one could be so valuable as he.

He quickly explained his plan. His destination, of course, was Fort Dinwiddie, and he intended to journey far enough to the northward to avoid the Nippinocks. Still the latter would soon learn of the flight of the little party and would do their utmost to cut off their escape. It was quite certain they would suspect the strategy of the Mingo and therefore try to checkmate it.

Logan would take the lead and he gave the order

in which he was to be followed,—Arthur first, Aunt Cynthia second, and Stanton last. They were to keep as near one another as possible, step softly, avoid speaking, and leave everything to him. While these preliminaries were being arranged, Arthur ventured to ask:

"Suppose one of us hears or sees something that you don't notice, what shall he do?"

The Mingo quietly replied:

"You won't see or hear anything that Logan don't notice."

Stanton chuckled, and Aunt Cynthia in a sharp undertone ordered him to keep quiet. The Mingo, conceiving he had said enough, immediately began the journey that was to prove more strangely eventful than any member suspected.

Now, it will be perceived, it was all-important that our friends should make all the progress they could while the night lasted. The Nippinocks could by no possibility learn the course they had taken until daylight, and therefore pursuit was out of the question until after the sun rose.

Much has been written about the amazing skill of the American Indian in trailing a fugitive through the unbroken forest, but there was little or no fear of anything of the kind in the present instance. The trailing of a party is effective when a long distance is traversed, and there is no call for special haste.

But the work before our friends was very hard, for throughout most of the distance there was nothing in the nature of a path or trail of which they could take advantage. The reader has already learned something of the difficulties in the shape of rocks, bowlders, undergrowth, gulches, and roughness of the ground, whose slopes were at every angle. The gloom was so deep that the Mingo was often compelled to keep within arm's reach of Arthur Oakland, while in the more open spaces a distance of a rod or more separated them.

Logan was too considerate to forget Aunt Cynthia, who was wholly unaccustomed to this sort of work. Had she been absent, he would have pressed the boys to the utmost, but he frequently paused on her account, perhaps touched by her grim, uncomplaining silence. After a time they came to a small natural opening, or clearing, where the four sat down, side by side, on a fallen oak, and the Mingo perpetrated one of his rare jokes.

"We go no farther till daybreak."

"You need n't think I 'm tired," snapped Aunt Cynthia; "I 'll let you know when I need rest; why won't we go any farther until daybreak?"

"We can't," gravely replied Logan.

"Why can't we?"

"It 's daybreak now."

The boys chuckled so loudly that the indignant

Aunt Cynthia whirled about and gave Stanton, who was nearest her, such a vigorous box that he tumbled over backward, with his feet pointing toward the sky. She was reaching beyond him to serve Arthur in the same manner, when he toppled over and kicked harder than his cousin.

"I guess it was the wind of your hand, aunty," he said, forgetting the previous instructions of the Mingo, who must also have forgotten them, for he looked on the scene smiling and amused and without reproof.

When the boys deemed it safe, they meekly climbed back to their seats on the log, furtively watching their aunt, and keeping a safe distance from her.

Logan had spoken truly, for the growing light in the wood showed that the eventful night was at an end. They had been laboring through the forest for a number of hours, but had penetrated only a few miles, mainly due to the consideration shown to the female member of the company.

Seated thus, the guide made no objection to a brief conversation, and in fact he started one by turning to Arthur with the question, meant for both boys:

"Are my sons hungry?"

Before they could reply, Aunt Cynthia responded in her characteristic manner:

"What a foolish question! Of course they're hungry; they're *always* hungry!"

"We can't help it, aunty; we were born that way."

"And it keeps growing on you; I never saw your equal."

No doubt the strange escape of the party put all in fine spirits, the Mingo himself sharing the general good-nature.

"I'm willing to wait till we get to the fort before eating," added Aunt Cynthia, "if we're a week on the road."

The boys groaned, and Arthur said:

"We'll die with hunger, if we have to wait more than a day longer; how long can *you* stand it, Logan?"

"Not more than two or three weeks," he gravely replied.

The youths stared at each other in dismay; their thoughts were unutterable.

The Mingo rose to his feet and looked keenly about him. Then, pointing to the farther side of the small open space, he said:

"Brook over there,—drink while I go away for a little while; I soon come back, and," he added impressively, "don't talk loud; *don't shoot gun!*"

They assured him his commands should be obeyed, and without another word he moved off as silently as a shadow and disappeared in the forest.

Left to themselves, the three walked the short distance to the point indicated by the Mingo, where, as he informed them, they found a small brook of cold, clear water, from which all drank, after which they laved their faces and hands, Aunt Cynthia's apron serving as a towel for each, for pocket-handkerchiefs were almost unknown among the usual class of boys in colonial times.

CHAPTER XXXII

AN EARLY CAMP

AUNT CYNTHIA and the two boys walked thoughtfully back to the fallen tree, upon which they seated themselves as before. The youths recalled the invariable custom at each of their homes, and neither was surprised when their relative drew her Bible from her pocket, and without speaking handed it to Arthur Oakland.

He knew what she meant, for he had thus been called upon by his own parents, and by his uncle and aunt when visiting them. He opened the sacred volume, and turning over the leaves for a moment, read in a subdued, reverential voice, the one hundred and forty-fifth psalm, the closing words of which impressed all with their beautiful appropriateness:

"The Lord upholdeth all that fall, and raiseth up all those that be bowed down.

"The eyes of all wait upon thee; and thou givest them their meat in due season.

"Thou openest thine hand, and satisfiest the desire of every living thing.

"The Lord is righteous in all his ways, and holy in all his works.

"The Lord is nigh unto all that call upon him, to all that call upon him in truth.

"He will fulfil the desire of them that fear him: He also will hear their cry, and will save them.

"The Lord preserveth all them that love him: but all the wicked will he destroy.

"My mouth shall speak the praise of the Lord: and let all flesh bless his holy name forever and forever."

At the conclusion of the reading, Arthur closed the volume, and, still holding it in his hand, he knelt down with the others by the fallen tree, while the aunt uttered a simple, touching prayer, thanking their Heavenly Father for the protection He had extended over them, entreating Him to deliver them out of the perils by which they were encompassed, and to cheer the hearts of the dear ones who were sorrowing for them. Though the boys were silent during the petition, they prayed as fervently in spirit as the good woman kneeling between them.

Then they talked together, kindly and affectionately, and with nothing trivial in their words or thoughts. Thus far they had had a wonderful deliverance from dangers when it seemed that only a miracle could save them. They were deeply grateful to the only One who could thus extricate them from the labyrinth of peril, and their faith was strong that the same hand would sustain and lead them through the trials yet to come.

Knowing nothing except in a general way of the attack that was to be made upon the settlement, they felt no special solicitude for their friends; but, when they reflected how anxious or distressed those friends were for them, they sympathized and were troubled on account of the same.

There was more than one occurrence of the preceding few hours which puzzled them, especially that withdrawal of the small party besieging the cabin, so as to permit the unmolested departure of the inmates.

"I suppose Logan will explain it when he gets ready," said Stanton, "But how is it to be explained that he went out to fight Ooromoo, who was eager to fight him; and yet, though the two met, they did n't try to hurt each other, but parted as if they were friends; I wonder if they *did* become friends."

"No, for that is n't Indian nature," said Arthur; "they are bitter enemies and will always be so."

"Why, then, did n't they fight?"

"I don't understand it, and therefore can't answer you; what do you think, aunty?"

She shook her head.

"I have given that matter little thought, but perhaps their hearts were softened. You know I have talked very plainly to Logan and I boxed Ooromoo's ears because he dared to say 'damn' in my presence. I am hopeful the two remembered my instructions."

The simplicity of this declaration caused the boys to glance slyly at each other, but they made no comment and their aunt continued:

"Some folks maintain that the days of miracles are past, but they are wrong."

"Why are you so sure of that, aunty?" respectfully asked Stanton.

"Have we not been saved by a miracle, as true a one as that which rescued Brookfield, in Massachusetts, when the rain descended just in time to save the blockhouse which the Injins had shoved a load of hay against and set fire to?"

"That *was* one of the strangest things that happened during King Philip's War," said Arthur, "but Logan hasn't told us as yet why the Nippinocks left when they did."

"Maybe they did not leave; it may be they were stricken with blindness like Saul of Tarsus when on the road to Damascus."

"I don't think it was that, aunty," said Stanton gently; "I never heard of a blind Indian."

"What was it then:

"Let us wait till Logan is ready to tell us. I wonder where he is gone?" and the boys looked around as if expecting to see him emerge from the wood, for day was fully come.

"I suspect he is looking for a spot that will give him a view of the country in front and behind us. He said the Nippinocks were on every side, and when they learn that we have left our home you can be sure they will make a keen hunt for us, and Logan does n't mean to take any chances that he does n't have to take."

An hour passed and there was no sign of Logan. The bright autumn sun climbed the sky, bringing a day as crisp, clear, and beautiful as that which preceded it, and the same profound stillness reigned over mountain, stream, and forest. No sound of gun or cry of animal reached their ears. It was as if they were the only living persons in the heart of a limitless solitude.

None of the party had slept for twenty-four hours, and the boys, tired and drowsy, slid down beside the log, laid their heads against the shaggy bark, and glided into dreamland. Although she had been deprived of slumber as long as they, Aunt Cynthia was as alert and wide awake as if she had arisen from a night's peaceful slumber.

She looked at the unconscious boys, clothed in homespun, the pictures of rugged health and youthful strength. The lips of each were parted so as to give a glimpse of the even white teeth, and the tint of the pearl showed in the centre of their cheeks, which glowed with life and overflowing spirits; and, though the face of Aunt Cynthia was stern and hard, and bitter words often fell from her lips, yet something like a tear now shone in each eye as she gazed silently upon the youths.

One was motherless, and the parent of the other was Aunt Cynthia's own sister, yet neither of those two ever loved the boys more than she. True she scolded them and not infrequently they felt the weight of her hand, but that she esteemed her peculiar privilege, and she would have been quick to resent any such discipline from others, except their own parents. She would not submit in silence to hear them censured, and had she chosen to express her honest opinion of them (which nothing could persuade her to do in their hearing) it would have been:

"They are the best, the most manly, and noblest boys that live anywhere; there was never any so handsome as they, and deny it if you dare!"

As for the big sturdy fellows themselves, they fully returned the affection of Aunt Cynthia, and they would have wept over her loss as if she were their own mother.

Thus alone, as it were, in the depth of the great wilderness, the woman again drew forth her Bible and began reading it. The precious volume was her daily companion, and she found in it that sweet comfort which it never fails to yield to every son and daughter of man, no matter how deep his sorrow or affliction. She was thus engaged, when a slight rustling caused her to look up. The boys were wide awake and standing on their feet.

"How long have we been asleep, aunty?" asked Arthur.

"More than an hour," was her reply.

"And Logan has n't come back; I always feel as if something had happened to him when he overstays his time. He is the smartest Indian that ever lived, but there must be a last time with him."

"He did n't say when he would return; if you feel so worried, you 'd better go and look for him."

Arthur glanced at his cousin.

"There 's danger all around us, Stant; if we wait here, the Indians are sure to find us; we are as safe on the road as in this place."

"So I think; Logan did n't order us to stay where we are; he said he would soon come back, and we must n't fire our guns; I 'm sure he would have been here before this unless something had gone wrong; let 's take a look and see how the land lies."

Aunt Cynthia made no objection, but resumed reading her Bible as if the matter was settled.

"Yonder is a high ridge," added Arthur, indicating a steep rocky and wooded elevation a short distance to the north; "while you pass over to the left of that pile of rocks I will turn to the right, and we'll both make a study of all the country we can see; I shouldn't be surprised if we are able to catch sight of Fort Dinwiddie."

"We don't expect to be away long," said Stanton to their relative, who merely nodded her head and continued reading, apparently without the slightest misgiving concerning them or herself. The ridge to which Arthur had referred was a little more than a hundred yards distant and sloped upward for about the same distance, when it terminated in a wooded crest, broken by so many rocks, bowlders, and ravines that its wildness would have repelled any one not so accustomed to mountain-climbing as our two young friends.

Agreeably to Arthur's suggestion, they parted company at the base of the ridge, he turning to the right, while his companion diverged to the left. They immediately lost sight of each other, and did not expect to meet again until they did so in the presence of Aunt Cynthia.

"I don't know whether this is the best thing to do," mused Arthur, as he picked his way with extreme caution around bowlders, between rocks, and along deep, ravine-like depressions, peering, listening, and often pausing in his guarded ascent; "but Logan can't find much fault, for he didn't forbid it, and I don't like the idea of sitting still and doing nothing. If we three have got to strike out for Warrenburg alone, we can't start any too soon."

Nothing was seen or heard until very near the summit. The ascent was so steep and rough that, toughened and hardened as were the youth's muscles, some of his halts were as much for rest as for the purpose of observation. Nothing, we say, occurred to cause misgiving until near the crest of the ridge, and he was already speculating as to the extent of the view that was to reward him, when he found himself in the most startling peril that mind can conceive.

CHAPTER XXXIII

HIDE AND SEEK WITH DANGER

ARTHUR OAKLAND, firmly grasping his rifle, had paused on the edge of a gorge fully thirty feet deep, which opened so suddenly before him that he would have been precipitated over the edge had he not been advancing with great caution and deliberation. The chasm looked as if some great convulsion of nature had rent the mass of stone apart, throughout an extent of several hundred feet.

When a person comes upon such a check his first feeling is that it is of the utmost importance that he shall lose no time in placing himself on the other side. Such was Arthur's impulse, and, standing close to the edge, he measured the intervening space with his eye, and asked himself whether by taking a short run he could not leap across. A glance to the right showed a widening of the chasm, so it was useless to seek in that direction. Turning his eye to the left, he could not note any perceptible difference in the width, but, as he shifted his head without moving his body, he became aware that a shadowy figure was stealing upon him from the rear with the silence of a shadow.

The situation could not have been more terrifying for the warrior was advancing absolutely without noise, and must reach the lad in the course of a few moments. He could have slain him before this with rifle, tomahawk, or knife, and the fact that he had not done so made it evident that he intended either to grapple with him, or—what seemed more likely— push him suddenly over the ledge to the bottom of the rocky ravine, with the certainty that he would be killed or dreadfully injured by the fall.

That which Arthur Oakland did was the prompting of an intuition which often comes to one without reasoning, and is nothing less than a providential direction as to the right course to follow in some great crisis. There was time for him to whirl about and fire upon his stealthy foe, but he made no move to do so and remained as motionless as a statue. He did not even turn his head, but seemed to be gazing steadily to the left, as if studying the width of the ravine some distance away. While doing this, his insidious enemy was in his field of vision, and every foot of his progress was followed with the eye.

On the part of the Indian, he observed as a matter of course the turning of the head of the youth, but he could not know whether he had discovered the approach of the danger. The fact that the boy did not betray the least excitement, but continued gazing steadily to the left, must have convinced the warrior that he suspected nothing of his peril.

The Nippinock silently diverged a little to the right, so as to get out of the field of vision, but he failed to do so. Arthur noted everything, and, unsuspicious as he seemed to be, his senses were on the alert and his muscles were so braced that they were like steel.

Less than a dozen paces away, the Indian's crouching posture became nearly upright, and with several short, noiseless steps he ran forward, and thrusting out both hands, one of which held his rifle, gave a bounding push at the body of the boy, who at precisely the right second whisked to one side and offered just enough free, unobstructed space for the Nippinock to shoot over the edge of the gorge, which he proceeded to do, and with outstretched hands in front of him went sprawling to the bottom.

Arthur stepped to the edge and peered over.

"A pretty clever trick," he muttered, "even if it is my own, and it saved my breaking the order of Logan not to fire my gun. I guess that fellow won't try any more business like that—I am not so sure, either."

To his amazement the warrior, instead of being killed by the fall, did not seem even to be seriously hurt. In some way he managed to save himself, for hardly had he landed, when he rose to his feet, turned his head, and looked upward, as if to learn how it all happened. There is no explaining the waggery of the American boy, nor the time and circumstances under which it will manifest itself. Standing on the upper edge of the ravine, and looking down upon the Nippinock, Arthur Oakland deliberately bowed low in mock obeisance and made a military salute, immediately stepping back out of sight, and it was well, perhaps, that he did so, for there are some insults which even the American Indian cannot brook.

But with all the youth's whimsicalities, he had too much rugged sense to neglect the important duty that had brought him hither. He had not yet made his survey of the surrounding country nor settled whether it was best for him and his companions to push on homeward without awaiting the return of the Mingo. The cousins had separated so as to gain a more extended view, but Arthur now determined to rejoin Stanton, for he felt that if Logan should come back while they were absent—and nothing was more probable than that he would do so—he would be displeased and might find his plans seriously interfered with.

So Arthur began picking his way along the rocky ridge toward the left, with the purpose of rejoining

Stanton Bothwell, who could not be very far away. With all his training in the ways of the woods, Arthur lost sight, however, of one fact: that was the likelihood of the baffled Nippinock's returning to revenge himself upon the one who had so cleverly outwitted him, and yet that is precisely what took place.

At the end of ten or fifteen minutes, Arthur had reached a point which he believed must be in the neighborhood of Stanton. It was as rocky and wooded as the portion he had just left, and he paused to look and listen. Although he had received so many proofs of the presence of enemies on every hand, he failed to catch the first sign of life in any direction.

Standing motionless, he emitted the low, guarded, tremulous whistle which the cousins often used in communicating when in a situation of danger. The reply was prompt, but altogether different from what he expected.

From a huge bowlder, less than twenty yards away, Stanton Bothwell stepped out into view, and as he did so he held his rifle to his shoulder and aimed directly at Arthur Oakland!

Before the astounded youth could ask the meaning of the startling action, his cousin called:

"*Stand a little aside, Art, so I can make sure of him!*"

Quick to comprehend the meaning of this command, Arthur leaped like a flash to the right. His cousin still held his weapon levelled, but did not press the trigger. Instead of doing so, he shook with suppressed laughter, but did not once lower his gun.

The explanation was clear. The Nippinock was still stealing up behind the youth who had used him so ill, confident of having his victim entrapped, but not quite ready to strike, when, presto! beyond that victim there suddenly stepped into sight a second lad, whose rifle was aimed straight at the warrior.

Never was there a more decisive instance of one person "getting the drop" on another. Fully armed as was the warrior, any hostile movement that he might make would be instantly anticipated by the young man who commanded the situation. The throwing up of the hands in token of surrender is unknown among the aborigines, and really there was but one thing left for this dusky miscreant to do, and he did it with promptness and dispatch.

In a panic of dread, he whirled about and ran for life,—dodging from right to left in the weak hope of disconcerting the aim of his foe, and whisking behind the rocks and out of sight on the first opportunity. He made such a grotesque figure that Stanton Bothwell could not help laughing, while Arthur did not fully grasp the situation until the red man had disappeared. Then he asked:

"Why did n't you shoot, Stant?"

"I had two reasons: Logan cautioned us against it, and then there was no need of it. That fellow is so scared he won't get over it for a month. *He* won't bother us any more."

"But he will let the others know."

"Logan must attend to that. Why did n't you look behind you now and then, when you were coming this way?"

"I ought to have done so, but I thought I was through with *that* particular Indian."

And then Arthur related the occurrence with which the reader is familiar.

"A pretty close shave," was the comment of Stanton; "but how do you know this warrior is the same fellow? when they are in their war-paint I can't see any difference between them."

"I had a pretty fair view of him and am sure it is the one who meant to shove me over into the gorge; but what 's the odds? I have n't had a chance of studying the country and finding out what is the best for us to do."

"I have."

"What is it?"

"Go back to aunty."

"And why do that?"

"Logan must have returned by this time; if he has done so, he has made up his mind as to what course to follow, and, if so, he won't wait for us."

"He won't feel like doing so, but aunty may *make* him wait."

"She has a will of her own, and sometimes Logan acts as if he was afraid of her, but he has shown, too, that when he has made up his mind she has to do as he says."

The decision of Stanton Bothwell was so prudent that his cousin could offer no objection, and the two began picking their way down the ridge toward the opening where they had left their relative a short time before. Their recent experience made them extremely cautious, for they needed no reminder that danger was on every hand. Indeed, they reproached themselves for having left their aunt wholly alone, though in doing so they followed her advice.

It proved as they anticipated. A few minutes later, when they joined Aunt Cynthia, she was seen talking with the Mingo, who stood calmly in front of her, while she remained seated on the log. Looking at the two, one would never have supposed that a thought of danger had entered either head. The Mingo looked sternly at the boys as they approached and demanded why they had gone away even for a short time. They made a frank explanation, but he showed no interest in their adventure, and it was plain he was dissatisfied with their conduct. He made no comment, however, beyond:

"Bad—very bad; we must hurry,—don't talk,—don't shoot gun,—follow Logan, — step soft like fawn."

There could be no doubt that the Mingo had delayed the start until the return of the boys, and, as it came out, he did so without any appeal from Aunt Cynthia. He would have been willing that the boys should suffer for their disregard of his wishes, but not to the extent of losing their lives. He would cut a sorry figure escorting the aunt to her relatives with word that he had virtually abandoned her nephews in their extremity!

The immediate vicinity of the clearing had been trodden by so many different persons that the hostiles would make no attempt to trail the fugitives, but the Nippinocks would scatter through the wilderness, so as to make sure they interposed between them and the settlement, and, calling into play their well-known skill, they could hardly fail to locate the little party, even though they were under the guidance of Logan the Mingo; for, if it be true that some things can be done as well as others, it is none the less true that some things cannot be done any more than others.

The problem confronting Logan has already been made clear, it being simply to guide his friends through the wilderness to Fort Dinwiddie in the face of the dread obstacles in his path. The fugitives never could have done it unassisted, and it remained to be seen whether they could do it with the help of the Mingo.

The latter understood the art of obliterating his footprints so as to baffle one of his own race, but there was no way of hiding those of two boys and a woman. The encounter of the cousins with the Nippinock promised to complicate matters, for, despite the panic in which the warrior fled, nothing was more certain than that he would soon communicate what he had learned to his companions, who would find little difficulty in locating the trail of the party, which being done, they would follow it with the persistency of bloodhounds.

It was more than a score of miles to the first point of real safety, over the circuitous route Logan was following, and, there being no path of which they could take advantage, it would consume the better part of the day to accomplish the journey.

All were a-hungered, but the Mingo, so far as he himself was concerned, could have gone a day or two longer without inconvenience. It was impossible to obtain any game, nor would they have dared to kindle a fire if meat had been at command; but the woods abounded with different kinds of nuts of which the three ate as they walked.

"This sort of thing will do so long as we can't get anything better," said Stanton as he cracked a "shellbark" as if it were a peanut between his strong teeth; "but if we ever reach home won't we bring up the average, Art?"

"More than likely we 'll go a good deal ahead of it; poor Logan does n't seem to be troubled with any appetite at all."

"He has just as big an appetite as we, but somehow or other he knows how to boss it, while ours bosses us."

There was not a square rod of ground between the clearing and the settlement with which the Mingo was not familiar. It has been explained that most of the region was mountainous and wild, containing many caverns and rocky recesses which would serve admirably as temporary defences, where the little party could hold ten times their number at bay.

But this of necessity could be for only a short time, for our friends would be without food or water; but Logan counted upon those at the settlement (who must be greatly concerned for their safety) learning of their plight and coming to their rescue. That a collision with the Nippinocks would take place he looked upon as equally certain as the shining of the sun overheard.

A most disquieting feature of the situation was that the nearest spot which could be made to serve as a means of defence was a half-mile distant. If overtaken before that point was attained, it was all up with the party.

No wonder, therefore, that Logan was grave and anxious when he faced eastward and warned his companions that all talking must cease, that they must walk rapidly, and keep as near him as possible. He took the lead, hardly pausing to push aside the bushes that obtruded in his front, gliding around rocks and bowlders, passing between trees, climbing sharp declivities, checking his speed in going down steep places,—doing it all, as it seemed, with utter carelessness and indifference, and yet rarely making a noise that was perceptible to those who were almost treading on his heels.

Every few minutes he stopped and glanced around, even among the tree branches, and as all stood in silence, the Mingo listened, but half the distance to the natural refuge was passed without the trained eye or ear discovering anything to cause alarm.

It was at this juncture that Logan made a change in the order of advance. He passed to the rear, leaving the relative positions of the others as before. His friends suspected this was because that point had become the position of known danger, but none questioned their guide.

Technically, therefore, Arthur Oakland became

leader of the little company. Looking at the Mingo, he asked in an undertone:

"What am I to do, Logan?"

"Go straight on; turn not to the right or left; *walk faster.*"

It was enough, and the youth pushed ahead at a walk that rose almost to a trot. The way was rough, uneven, and difficult, but he pressed vigorously forward, and the energetic Aunt Cynthia did not lag or fall behind, while Stanton Bothwell kept within arm's length of her. Each boy carried his rifle in a trailing position, for he instinctively felt that peril brooded in the air about them.

When the fugitives had gone a few rods, Arthur looked back. The Mingo was standing like a statue, his head turned away, scrutinizing the wood to the rear, with all his senses keyed to the highest point.

Young Oakland did not pause, but, noting that his friends were with him, pressed swiftly on, heeding the orders of Logan to make his course direct. A little farther and he looked back again. The Mingo was invisible, not because he had changed his position, but the three had passed beyond sight of him.

Suddenly Aunt Cynthia touched the arm of her nephew, and he looked around.

"Arthur, you are turning to the left," she whispered.

"That's so," added Stanton in the same guarded voice.

The lad had no way of making certain, but, accepting the warning of his friends, he shifted his course to the right, taking pains to do so only to a slight extent. He knew not whither he was going, but, like a true soldier, obeyed orders.

In truth, he was hurrying due eastward, not because it was the direct route to the settlement, but because it led straight to the mass of tumbled rocks where the Mingo believed they must make their final stand.

Suddenly the spiteful crack of a rifle sounded from the rear. Either Logan or an enemy had discharged his weapon, but the fugitives knew better than to stop to investigate. The report of the gun was not accompanied by the outcry which almost invariably marks the fatal wounding of an American Indian, and such as would have been the case had the Mingo fallen. From this fact, his friends hoped—if the weapon were levelled at him—it had missed its aim.

Arthur caught his foot in a running vine, and, despite his desperate efforts to recover himself, fell on his hands and knees, his gun flying from his grasp.

"Mercy, Arthur! are you hurt?" asked his frightened aunt, forgetting everything else in her anxiety

Hide and Seek with Danger 287

for the boy, who was on his feet in an instant, weapon in hand.

"No!" he answered, as he sped onward again.

It would seem that if Logan had not been harmed, he would make haste to rejoin them after discharging his weapon. Both boys glanced backward, in obedience to the thought, but saw nothing of him.

"I wonder what's to be the end of this?" Arthur asked himself; "we can't keep it up all the way home, and, if the Indians are after us, they can run a mighty sight faster than we."

Nevertheless, there was no abatement of energy on the part of the fugitives, as they fought their way forward, all equally zealous and determined.

"Arthur, can't you go faster?" asked his aunt over his shoulder.

"Yes; can you?" he replied; "I shall have to run."

"Do so; I know something dreadful is going to happen."

Both boys were astonished that, despite the severe exertion which had continued some time, the lady's respiration showed no increase and she gave no evidence of fatigue.

Arthur changed his rapid walk to a trot, which the continually interposing obstacles compelled him to reduce to a much slower pace that he might force his way through dense undergrowth, climb some abrupt declivity, or pass around masses of stone, where he could not see a yard in advance.

It was extremely difficult to keep a direct course, but, with the aid of his companions, he was quite successful. The little party had almost passed the eighth of a mile of solitude, and were in the thickest part of a stretch of oaks, when Stanton called in a startled undertone:

"Look out, Art! there's some one ahead of you among the trees!"

His cousin had caught a glimpse of the figure, and, grasping the arm of his aunt, he drew her hastily to one side.

"Keep behind this trunk, aunty, or you will be shot!"

Then the manly fellow looked after his own safety. He leaped behind the nearest tree of suitable size and, turning his head, saw that his cousin had already done the same some paces distant, and was furtively peeping out in quest of a chance for a shot at their enemy, who, for the moment, was invisible.

CHAPTER XXXIV

STRANGE DOINGS

THE three had scarcely leaped into positions of safety, when Aunt Cynthia called in an excited undertone:

"Don't shoot! don't you see it is n't an Injin?"

The warning was in the nick of time, for Arthur Oakland was already sighting his rifle at a form dimly traceable among the undergrowth, when it came into distinct view, and the man, removing his cap, bowed low and said:

"It gives me great pleasure to greet my friends; I am zo happy and I place my poor zarvices at your deespozal."

The party in their astonishment forgot for the moment the imminent peril from which they were fleeing, and, coming out from behind the tree-trunks, where they had taken refuge, walked forward to greet the French officer, who stood, hat in hand, smiling and bowing, his last salutation being a profound one to Aunt Cynthia.

"We 're mighty glad to see you, Captain," said Stanton heartily; "you are the last person we expected to meet; where did you come from?"

"Ah, I go to ze reseedence and I finds you not; zen I sets out to look for you; ze woods have many Enjans, and zey, too, look for you; it is a most unhappy time, and I places my sword at your zarvice."

"We are not alone, Captain," said Aunt Cynthia; "we have a noble Injin,—a friend, Logan, who is trying to guide us to the settlement."

"I see him not," replied the officer, looking around; "why is he not here zat he may protect you?"

"He is not far away; he will soon be here; he is looking out for the Indians that are following us," explained Arthur.

"Ah, zey are ahead and to one side; I know not where to tell you to go. Ah, zere is one of ze devals now! Leave him to me!"

But it was the Mingo who was discerned at that moment, loping toward them with the noiselessness of a shadow. A glance at the uniformed Frenchman made the situation clear to Logan, who joined them a moment later, not slackening his speed until among them. He and the officer scanned each other closely, but there was scant time for explanation or meaningless words.

"Run!" said the Mingo; "the Nippinocks are close by! Don't wait!"

"Are we following the right course?" asked Arthur.

"Pretty near! I show the way! Come after me! Run fast!"

A single leap placed him at the head of the company, and conceiving that he had said enough he fell into his swinging lope again, Arthur, Aunt Cynthia, and Stanton following closely and keeping pace well with him.

Only two or three rods were run, when the Mingo stopped so suddenly that it required quick effort on the part of his friends to avoid running into him. He was looking to the rear and instinctively the others turned their eyes in that direction. Captain Choteau was seen standing with drawn sword, glancing vigilantly at the different points of the compass. Perceiving their action, he saluted with his sword and smiled as if on parade.

Logan beckoned with one hand for him to come after them, and Stanton said:

"Hurry, Captain! we have n't a minute to lose."

"I am at ze post of dutee," he replied; "I protects ze rear; I entreat you to hurry like ze dev— vary mooch; I stays here; I zalute you!"

And he made another military salutation and turned away to signify the argument was closed.

"What a brave man!" exclaimed Aunt Cynthia, while all were thrilled with admiration; "he means to stand there alone and fight all the Injins. It is a shame for us to let him do so. Arthur, you and Stanton run back and get hold of him and pull him along; we must not desert him."

"*Come!*" commanded the Mingo so sharply that no one dared disobey him. He struck his lope again, with his companions close upon his heels, and in less than a minute the whole party had passed out of sight of the brave officer, whom the last backward glance showed to be standing, sword in hand, as cool as a statue, looking steadily in the direction from which, as he had learned, the danger would first come.

It was a gallant act, and it did seem unfeeling to leave him thus alone, but so Logan willed, and no one dared gainsay him.

The party were close to the refuge which the Mingo had in mind, and where he expected to make his last stand, having become convinced that it would be certain destruction to press on when he was absolutely assured the Nippinocks were expecting such an attempt and had interposed across their path.

Perhaps two hundred yards beyond the point where the Captain was met the shelter was reached, and it proved to be of the most primitive nature. It was simply a pile of rocks, so tumbled together that a natural cavern was formed barely more than a dozen feet in the longest direction, and hardly half of that in width, and with a height still less.

The door was an irregular opening, perhaps a yard in extent. Since everything was solid stone, it will be perceived that the position was naturally a strong one, for two or three well-armed men could hold off a large force and at the same time keep themselves well screened against any fire from outsiders.

The fatal weakness of the defence has already been pointed out. None of the party had a mouthful of food, nor was it possible to obtain a drop of water. A besieging party had only to maintain its vigilance to compel the defenders to fall in time, like ripe fruit, into their hands.

Therefore the only purpose sought by the Mingo was temporary safety. The refuge once attained, the Nippinocks could be stood off until night, when he would make a desperate effort to get word to Fort Dinwiddie of the straits of the party and bring a strong force to their rescue. Logan himself looked upon this as impossible, nevertheless it was all that was left to him.

The moment the dark, cavernous opening was perceived, he pointed to it and said in his former peremptory manner:

"Go in!"

He was looking at Arthur when he spoke, and the youth obeyed without hesitation. The moment he started to do so, the Mingo glanced significantly at Stanton, who entered the opening almost at the same moment with his cousin. Then their guide turned to Aunt Cynthia and said firmly, but more gently:

"Go with them,—don't wait."

"I won't stir a step," she replied in her most decisive manner, "if you mean to desert Captain Choteau. What can one man do against all them scandalous villains?"

"What do you want Logan to do?" asked the Mingo, with an odd expression of countenance.

"Run back, pick him up, throw him over your shoulder, and bring him here! Never mind if he does kick and say bad words; will you do it?" she eagerly asked.

"Yes, Logan will do it if you go with my sons."

"That's a bargain!" replied the vastly relieved woman, who lost no time in joining her nephews, peeping out from the mouth of the cavern and wondering at the cause of the delay. When she had a chance to do the same, the Mingo was gone, and the boys had noticed that he ran back over his own trail. He had certainly taken the direction of Captain Choteau, but it is not to be supposed his intention was what he had announced to Aunt Cynthia, though for a time she firmly believed him.

Some minutes passed, during which the aunt and her nephews devoted their faculties to listening, and did not speak. Not even the twittering of a bird reached their ears. Each youth grasped his rifle, and was alert for the first sign of peril, for neither needed any instruction as to his duty.

With their nerves on edge, Stanton was the first to give way to impatience.

"I can't understand why Captain Choteau and Logan stay outside, while we are here. Logan was in a tremendous hurry to reach this place, and now does n't make any use of it."

"I was thinking the same thing," said Arthur; "we have plenty of room for him, and he must be in great danger out there,—and so is the Captain; but he does n't understand the ways of the woods like Logan."

"Did n't you hear what me and him said?" asked their aunt.

"We could n't catch it all."

"He promised to go back and bring Captain Choteau."

"The Captain won't come."

"Logan *promised* to bring him."

"He has had plenty of time; what will he do if the Captain refuses, as I know he will from the way he acted a little while ago?"

"Logan gave me his word that he would lift him

on his shoulder and bring him in," said Aunt Cynthia, as if that settled the question.

The boys glanced at each other, and, despite the gravity of the situation, smiled. It was plain that the delay was causing the lady misgiving, and some minutes later she said:

"I wonder if Logan was fooling me."

"Whether he was or not," replied Arthur, "he never will bring the Captain here, because he can't; he has a sword and is his own master."

Aunt Cynthia was silent a little while longer. She was thinking hard over a new scheme that had come into her mind. Finally she out with it:

"I tell you, boys, it won't do! It's wrong! I insist that you go after them both and tell them they *must* come here right off!"

The youths heard these words with consternation, but there was no mistaking their earnestness.

"That would never do, aunty," said Stanton; "Logan would be offended and would never forgive us. You know he was angry a little while ago when we left you."

"Is he more important than *me*? I'm already offended; I won't stand it!"

"That may be, but it can't be helped; Logan is master; we never would have been able to leave home but for him; we must obey him."

"He didn't tell you to stay here till he came back."

"But he expects it, as he did a while ago."

"How do you know he does? You have never disobeyed me *yet*," she added with biting sarcasm; "you run no risk, and I demand that you go."

Despite the preposterousness of the scheme, each youth began to ask himself whether it could not be carried out without undue risk to any one. What induced them to entertain the thought was that so much time had passed without showing any reason for believing any of the Nippinocks were near. They must have paused in their pursuit, and the boys could think of no cause why the Mingo and officer should not join them.

Had they taken a few minutes to consider the matter, they would have dismissed it as suicidal; but the confinement in the narrow space and the waiting without anything occurring were irksome.

"Suppose, aunty, I should go alone?" suggested Arthur.

"No; *both* must go, for, if the Captain is stubborn, Logan may need your help to bring him in."

"What do you say, Stant?"

"I don't know what to say; it isn't like it was a while ago, and there's no reason to believe the Nippinocks are near; it's only a little way to where we left the Captain, and it won't take us more than a few minutes to find out how the land lies; we shall be so close, Aunty, that if we see anything is wrong, we can be back in a jiffy."

"Let 's go! Come on!" exclaimed Arthur, yielding to his sudden impulse and creeping outside the cavern, where he rose to his feet. Stanton immediately joined him, and then the two proceeded to carry out a plan, which, in view of what had taken place only a short time before, was inexcusable in its rashness. It seemed that nothing remained to round out and complete the blunder, and yet the monumental culmination came a few minutes later.

No one of her sex could have been more conscientious than Aunt Cynthia, and for a time she enjoyed the sweet consciousness of having done a high though not specially pleasant duty. It was time the two men were at the shelter, and, since they delayed their coming, it was her province to remind them so forcibly of their remissness that they could not but obey her wishes.

"When they see the boys they will know I am alone, and all will hurry back as fast as they can. Who cares if Logan is offended? If he says anything to the boys they can lay it on me, 'cause I made them go, and he knows I 'm not afraid of him, if some people are."

She uttered an exclamation as a sudden idea flashed upon her. She thought it was an inspiration, when it was simply the crowning act of idiocy.

"Logan was mistaken; the Nippinocks he expected have not come; they are farther to the rear than he thought; they may come pretty soon, but we are throwing away precious minutes; I know the course to Warrenburg, and can go there as well as they; I won't wait for them; instead of my traipsing behind Logan and Arthur let them follow *me*."

Emerging, as had the boys, from the cavern, she stood a brief while and looked around and listened. She saw and heard nothing unusual, and a moment later began walking rapidly in the direction of Fort Dinwiddie.

CHAPTER XXXV

KNIGHT AND LADY

CAPTAIN EUGENE CHOTEAU was standing with drawn weapon, after the disappearance of his friends, when the very thing he expected took place.

On the back trail appeared three Nippinock warriors coming directly toward him. Beyond question, they had discovered and identified him before he saw them, else they would not have approached in so open a manner. They knew him as the friend of Lame Panther, Great Bear, and, indeed, the whole tribe, among whom he had spent several days. Was he not, therefore, an ally, anxious for the success of their schemes of evil against the English?

Each buck carried a rifle, tomahawk, and hunting-knife. The officer, sword in hand, calmly watched them as they came up and halted within arm's length. Only one of their number could make himself understood in broken English.

"Hooh, brudder, see palefaces go past?"

"Yez; zey go zat way," coolly replied the Captain, indicating the direction by extending the point of his weapon; "and it vaz one leetle while ago."

"Hooh! heap good!" grunted the pleased warrior, striding off, but the officer leaped like a cat in front of him and interposed his weapon.

"You cannot go; zey have ladee: no shentlemen vill disturb ze noble ladee; you must turn back and apologize."

Though the Nippinock may not have understood the chivalry of these sentences, he did understand that the Frenchman had dared to check him, and he was aflame with rage. The action of the white man told the story with equal emphasis to the other bucks. All three dropped their rifles and whipped out their long, keen hunting-knives, for they were the preferable weapons at close quarters. Thus the officer was assailed by three fierce men with knives, but bear in mind that he was the best swordsman in his regiment.

In such a battle much depends upon the one who is the first to attack, and the Captain's act was an illustration of David Harum's wisdom in advising a man to do others as they would do him and to do it first. The foremost Nippinock was in the act of leaping like a panther at the officer, when he was met midway by a lightning thrust; there was a vivid flash under his left shoulder-blade, as the point of the sword appeared for an instant and was withdrawn with a quickness that no eye could follow, and the buck slumped down in a heap, killed before he had time to make a single yawp.

But the other two warriors were upon the officer in a twinkling. Both, however, were in his field of vision, and, like the skilled pugilist, he noted every movement. Leaping a single pace backward, he darted forward again, as if feet and limbs were made of rubber, and, parrying the blow of one, he ran him through with the same marvellous celerity and seeming lack of effort as at first.

Quick as he was, Captain Choteau was unable to parry the blow of the third, though his own weapon had been extracted in the fractional part of a second; but the amazing swordsman gave an example of dodging which no person could have surpassed. The panting savage, his painted face agleam with ferocity, struck viciously, and the officer heard the whizz of the knife that almost grazed his cheek.

The failure of the blow gave him the opening needed, and before the Nippinock could recover himself he sprawled forward and departed this life precisely as his predecessors had done. The whole three had been slain with incredible quickness, the strange combat having opened and closed within an interval of time that was less than three minutes!

The Captain plunged the matchless blade several times into the moist earth to the hilt to cleanse it of its crimson stains, and the next moment after withdrawing it he, too, fell suddenly forward on his face and did not stir, for he had caught sight of a fourth Indian hurrying to the spot. Although the Captain had his pistol at command, his dread was that this new enemy would call his rifle into play. His purpose, therefore, in falling was to give the impression that he had been mortally hurt, in order to draw the buck within reach of his sword.

Therefore he lay motionless, but with his weapon tightly grasped, and his half-closed eyes watching for his enemy, whose hurried footsteps he could easily trace over the pattering leaves. Let him but come within eight or ten feet, and the seemingly dead man would dart forward and bore him through before he could draw his hunting-knife.

The ruse succeeded. The Indian continued to advance until within the distance named, when he stopped, as if astounded at sight of the four lifeless forms stretched before him. Suddenly, without warning, one of them seemed to be hurled forward, as if shot from the mouth of a giant piece of ordnance, and crouching, like the very concentration of fury, with sword rigidly grasped, he aimed for his new antagonist.

But this time the Indian was as agile as he, and, leaping lightly aside, looked wonderingly at him, without attempting to use knife or tomahawk.

"A thousand pardones!" called the Captain with his old smile and courteous bow. "I did not obzarve zat it vos my friend Logaine; I crave your pardone."

The Mingo looked in amazement at the picture. Never before had he seen anything like it. Three men slain in the twinkling of an eye, without the use of firearms, without the least outcry, and with no harm to the man who had performed the astounding feat!

And the wonderful swordsman stood smiling, bowing, and humbly begging his pardon for his mistake as to the Indian's intentions.

"You do *that?*" asked Logan, quickly recovering himself, his astonishment still showing through the paint on his countenance.

"I do zat," replied the officer, with another bow, his white teeth gleaming under his mustache; "it vos, do you not zink,—vat you call him?—*arteestic?*"

"Has my brother no hurt?" asked Logan.

Having cleaned his sword, Captain Choteau shoved it into his scabbard, and now slowly and deliberately made a complete circuit on his heels, bringing all his body under inspection.

"Obzarve, my freend Logaine, vot you zee."

It was plain to the Mingo that the officer had not so much as a scratch, not even a rent of his coat or trousers showing. Henceforward, he was sure of the unbounded admiration of Logan.

"How iz ze noble ladee?" asked Captain Choteau, with much seriousness; "I hopes she bears ze fateeg of zis journey well. Ah, she is a noble ladee."

The Mingo did not quite follow the remarks of the Captain, but he said:

"She made me come back to help you fight. Hooh! you don't need help."

"I am mooch pleased zat zis leetle affaire take place not in her presence,—for it cause her one great zschock. My friend Logaine will be zo good zat he say nozzing to ze noble ladee; her nerves may not stand it; vill my good friend Logaine obleege?"

The Mingo understood the meaning of his friend and signified that he would respect his wishes, though it was with a mental reservation. No person is fonder of boasting than the American Indian, but none the less he respects modesty in a true and tried warrior.

It came out in the conversation which followed that the affair described had wrought an important change in the situation. Logan knew that he and his friends were hotly pursued by a number of Nippinocks, and his purpose in lingering at the rear was to hold this party in check until his friends could reach the refuge described. It has been shown that

Captain Choteau took the task off his hands and performed it to the queen's taste.

Had the three hostiles caught sight of the fugitives, there must have been an exchange of shots, and, encumbered as the latter were with the woman, the risk of such an encounter in the open must be avoided at all costs. Hence, the desperate and fortunately successful efforts of our friends.

But the peril was merely postponed for a brief time. Had the Nippinocks already removed as factors in the problem located the whites, they would have called others of their comrades to the spot, and the situation would have assumed the form already named. All this, however, was averted by the superb performance of Captain Choteau.

The question now was whether the party, strengthened through the addition of the officer, should hold the fort until night, or press forward at once with the certainty of another and perhaps more formidable encounter with the Nippinocks. The Captain insisted upon leaving the question to the Mingo, while he, stirred by admiration for his new ally, was equally insistent that he should express his views, and the curious discussion was under way when, to the amazement of both, Arthur Oakland and Stanton Bothwell appeared on the scene.

A glance revealed that their aunt was not with

them, and Logan demanded the meaning of their extraordinary action. It was Arthur who made the explanation.

Never before or afterward did any of the party witness such a scene as followed. Logan was beside himself with wrath. The gleam of his black eyes, and the tremor of his hand, as he placed it on his hunting-knife, left no doubt that his fury over this disregard of his wishes was so intense that he was ready to visit the final punishment upon the boys.

They never suspected their frightful peril, but Captain Choteau saw it, and grasped the hilt of his sword, ready to flash it out and anticipate the first action of the Mingo. Had the attack been made, there can be no doubt, in view of what has been recorded, that Logan would have perished then and there, as if smitten by a lightning stroke.

He did not carry out his fearful design, abandoning it not through personal fear, but because he quickly regained control of himself and thought better. Without uttering a word, he strode in the direction of the cavern, the others following silently and paying no heed to the shuddering proof of Captain Choteau's swordsmanship which they left behind them.

The cousins were depressed, for a realizing sense of their great blunder had come to them, and each was at a loss to understand why they allowed themselves to be influenced by the whim of their aunt.

"I hope nothing has happened to her," said Stanton, in an undertone to his cousin.

"What *could* happen? We have been gone only a little while, and whatever danger there was came from the rear, and Captain Choteau has attended to *that.*"

"Look at Logan!"

They had come in sight of the cavern, and the Mingo was seen to stop, partly bend his head, and peer in. Then he went closer that he might see better, and almost in the same second leaped back as if from before the muzzle of a levelled rifle. Darting his penetrating glances here and there, he said in his sepulchral voice:

"*She is gone!*"

All three stood speechless. There was no questioning the word of Logan, who, fortunately for himself and the boys, was partly expecting something of the kind, and had regained supreme mastery of his rage. In fact, he believed that Aunt Cynthia had ridden herself of the company of the boys for the purpose of gaining this chance of continuing her flight by herself.

His theory was that she knew she was a burden, but, moreover, was confident she could get on as well without as with them. She was familiar with the course to the settlement, and there was all the daylight she needed. Why, therefore, should she dawdle away the time?

Such, we say, was the theory of the Mingo, but, if anything, it added to his misgiving, for he knew, beyond all peradventure, that she would be outwitted by the Nippinocks.

Arthur and Stanton looked at each other in dismay and did not dare trust themselves to speak. Captain Choteau, who had removed his hat in anticipation of saluting Aunt Cynthia, replaced it with the remark:

"I am disappointed, and I hopes ze ladee has not made le grand mistake in not waiting to bid us adieu: what zinks my friend Logaine?" he asked, with his bow and smile, as he turned toward the Mingo. But the latter was in too tumultuous a mood to tell his thoughts. Without any evidence that he had heard himself addressed, he began a scrutiny of the ground in front of the cavern.

He was hunting for the footprints of Aunt Cynthia, and, since she had made no effort to hide them, they were easily detected. He gave no attention to his companions, but they kept their eyes upon him and did not allow his slightest action to escape them.

Having identified the trail, Logan stood a minute or so, while he glanced ahead, following it with his eye as far as he could. Then he broke into a lope and paused again and went through the same scrutiny. The footprints ran surprisingly straight and proved that the woman, instead of advancing blindly, was following a definite course, and the Mingo did not doubt that he understood what it was.

She was trending a little to the northeast with the purpose of striking a well-marked path, two or three miles distant, which led directly to the settlement. So well convinced was Logan of this that he decided to make no attempt to follow her trail, which would have delayed his progress, but to head directly for the path, which undoubtedly was the destination of the fugitive.

Logan explained nothing of this to his companions, but, breaking into his habitual lope, left them to fall in and follow as they might choose.

It would seem that with the comparatively slight start of Aunt Cynthia, her pursuers ought soon to have overtaken her, but they did not, and when Logan, after going some distance, looked down at the ground, he observed nothing of the footprints, which was as he expected, since he was "cutting across lots" to strike the path to Fort Dinwiddie.

But a shock came to him a little way farther. He approached a small brook, which it was necessary to leap. Several feet of ground on both sides was moist, and there, directly in front of him, and where he expected nothing of the kind, were several impressions made by the shoes of Aunt Cynthia.

There could be no mistake about it. She wore an unusually small and shapely shoe that could be confounded with that of no one else's.

As the companions of Mingo came up he pointed to the footprints, as distinct as if they were cast in a mould. But it was not the sight of them which took away the breath of the boys, but the impressions of an Indian's moccasins at the side of those of Aunt Cynthia!

What did it mean?

Only one meaning was possible. Had the Nippinock been following the woman he naturally would have taken longer strides, but he would have stepped over her trail, wholly obliterating it at certain intervals. Had he been in advance of the woman she would have noted his tracks and turned aside; but the marks of the moccasins in every instance were a foot or more to the left of those made by the shoes.

Therefore, when Aunt Cynthia crossed this rivulet, the warrior was in her company. That which was inevitable had come to pass.

Logan stood for a few minutes sunk in thought, looking not at the footprints, but in the direction in which they led. His companions ventured to ask him several questions, but he did not answer. Suddenly he uttered an exclamation, meant for no one except himself, and dashed off at a speed which, despite the efforts of his friends to equal, quickly carried him beyond sight.

CHAPTER XXXVI

AUNT CYNTHIA IS ENCOURAGED IN THE GOOD WAY

LOGAN the Mingo read aright the motives of Aunt Cynthia in leaving the cavern the instant her nephews were beyond sight, and setting out to make the journey alone to the settlement.

As she viewed matters, the entire party, each of whom was well armed, having passed to the rear, would hold their pursuers in check. Why, therefore, should she remain where she was until they came up and she again became a hindrance to them? She could not avoid being such a hindrance, and she was able to travel as rapidly without as with them. She knew the course to the settlement, and she believed her friends by their action had opened the road for her. Her grave mistake was in not understanding that the danger in front was as great as ever, and that no such thing as an "open door" existed.

But, as we have seen, she made the start, and it must be admitted that she improved her time. Strong and active, she did not content herself with walking, but instantly broke into a moderate run that was as swift as the lope of the Mingo.

She knew that by bearing slightly to the northeast she ought to reach the regular path to the settlement a few miles away, after which nothing could be easier than the remainder of the walk to Warrenburg.

All went well for the first mile. The course was so rough that she was often compelled to go slowly, and carefully pick her way through undergrowth and around obstructions, but whenever the ground permitted she assumed the gait which prevented her friends gaining in the pursuit that began soon after her flight. For the time she was following nothing in the nature of a trail, but her woodcraft enabled her to maintain without deviation the course she had laid out for herself.

Aunt Cynthia had certainly gone through many trying experiences during the preceding day and night, but the greatest shock of her life came while pressing vigorously forward, inspired with hope that had scarcely a shadow of fear.

She was within three or four paces of a large oak, and had veered a little to the left with the purpose of passing it, when an Indian warrior stepped silently forth and confronted her. The sight was so startling that she recoiled with a half-repressed scream and threw up her hands in helpless dismay.

More alarming than all, the first glance at the tall, sinewy red man revealed that he was Ooromoo, the Nippinock, over whose painted visage a glow of exultation seemed to spread at the thought that the helpless woman who had put an outrage upon him was now in his power.

Yes; this was the terrible warrior whom she smote with the palm of her hand within her own home the night before, because he had dared to utter a displeasing exclamation in her presence. He was the Nippinock who went forth to meet Logan the Mingo in deadly combat, and who was hunting down the harried fugitives with the ferocious persistency of the bloodhound.

But the woman did not quail. While hurrying on, she continually sent up her prayers to heaven, and, with another mental ejaculation for protection, she bravely looked the warrior in the face and said:

"Well, Ooromoo, you may now kill me if you choose."

"Why I kill you?" he asked with the same singular expression on his face, which puzzled the woman.

"There isn't any reason why you should, but that doesn't make any difference to heathens like you."

"I no kill—*now*."

This was not reassuring, but it removed the fear of instant death and gave Aunt Cynthia further time for prayer. She was puzzled, but, expecting no mercy from the fierce warrior, was prepared to accept her doom with the bravery and resignation of one whose faith in heaven is unshakable.

"Where are the rest of your warriors, Ooromoo?"

"All around,—everywhere," he replied with a sweep of his arm; "go with me."

Inasmuch as there was nothing to be gained by refusal, the prisoner walked forward, the two side by side. With all the whimsical notions that often actuated Aunt Cynthia, she had too much sense to see the remotest chance of escaping from Ooromoo without the aid of her friends. Her hope was that during the interval for which her captor had spared her life Logan would manage to overtake them, though she could not shut her eyes to the fearful picture conjured up by Ooromoo's declaration that the woods were full of Nippinocks.

"I suppose," was her thought, "that he will take me to where some of his people are waiting, and then they will tie me to a tree and burn me to death. If it is the Lord's will, I shall not murmur, for better men and women than I have died at the stake——"

"St! quick! hide there!"

Ooromoo seized her arm and almost tumbled her over in his haste to force her behind a bowlder several paces distant. Aunt Cynthia had seen nothing, but she did not protest or make resistance. She crouched low as bidden, and he added, without looking toward her:

"Don't move; make no noise; wait till Ooromoo comes for you!"

And with this extraordinary warning, he strode out of sight almost immediately beyond the bowlders.

Aunt Cynthia had the curiosity of her sex, and when several minutes passed she ventured to peep timidly forth from behind the bowlder. Only a few rods distant three Nippinocks, one of them being Ooromoo, were talking together in such low tones that she could not catch the murmur of their voices. It so happened that her captor stood facing her, while she saw only the sides and the backs of the others.

Ooromoo was looking directly toward her and could not fail to observe the bonnet and upper part of her face. Afraid of displeasing him, she drew back her head with the determination to await his will, whatever it might be. The minutes seemed endless, but by and by a soft rustling was heard, and the Nippinock came around the bowlder, and, pausing a few paces distant, looked at her with his odd, unfathomable expression and said:

"Follow, but wait till I tell you."

He walked for perhaps a hundred feet, until he was nearly hidden from view, when he turned and beckoned to her. She understood the meaning of this action to be that she was to maintain the same distance between them, and she did her best to comply with the requirement.

But where were the other two Nippinocks? She could see nothing of them, and a strange question stirred her.

"Can it be that Ooromoo is acting as my friend? No; for he will never forgive me for boxing his ears, and yet I did right."

Now that there was so much interval between them, it occurred to the prisoner that she might take advantage of it by slipping aside at some favorable point and either hide herself or seek the settlement by a divergent route. The more she reflected upon the matter the more certain she felt of success.

She was restrained by the growing belief that Ooromoo, for some reason incomprehensible to her, was acting the part of a friend.

"At any rate," she reflected, "I will wait until he gives me reason to think different."

The Nippinock looked back every few minutes, as if to make sure she was following instructions. Where the ground made it necessary he waited until she drew nearer, but did not permit her to join him.

Ooromoo called all his superb woodcraft into play, and there was need of it, for, if he were really a friend, he was in continual danger of meeting some of his brother warriors. None of them would dream of suspecting him until the proof was before their eyes, and his aim was to prevent their receiving such proof.

A considerable distance was travelled in this fashion, when Aunt Cynthia, who scarcely removed her eyes from the picturesque figure in front, saw him suddenly turn and make several excited gestures. Without being certain of his meaning, she accepted his action as an order for her either to run or hide herself. She did the latter, and cringed behind the nearest tree, which, fortunately, was within arm's reach.

Recalling her former experience, she resolved to wait with patience until he either approached or called to her to resume her course.

An extraordinary experience followed. Not being permitted to look in advance, Aunt Cynthia cast a searching glance to the rear, and with a feeling of consternation observed an Indian warrior moving stealthily from tree to tree and steadily drawing nearer.

In her dismay she would have dashed from her concealment and run forward to claim the protection of Ooromoo, thus spoiling the remarkable policy under way, had not a gesture from the Indian at the rear drawn closer attention to him.

"My gracious!" she gasped, "it is Logan!"

Something that was going on at the front with Ooromoo compelled the Mingo to screen himself, but Aunt Cynthia saw the gleam of his white teeth as he smiled and made a motion of his hand to signify that everything was right.

Having assured the woman on that point, Logan cautiously withdrew for several rods, and then remained invisible.

"I never seen such queer doings," reflected Aunt Cynthia, "and I can't understand what it all means, but, as near as I can figure out, it is this: Ooromoo intends to be my friend, though it's contrary to my idea of Injin natur' that he ever could be. Logan has found that out and tells me to trust him, but Logan himself ain't so sartin, so he's going to hang round ready for Ooromoo if he tries to play any tricks—what does *that* mean?"

A low whistle trembled from the front, and when it was heard a second time the woman again peeped cautiously forth. The Nippinock was standing alone some twenty yards away, looking in her direction. The instant her head appeared he beckoned her to come forward, and inasmuch as he immediately resumed his own advance the relative distance between them was maintained.

Several times Aunt Cynthia looked behind her in quest of Logan, but he was not seen, though she could not doubt that he was near at hand.

"It's a great comfort to know I have a friend both at the front and rear, though I can't feel real sartin of Ooromoo, but I guess he's what he pretends, for it would take a smarter Injin than him to fool Logan, and *he* does n't seem to have any doubt —at least not much—of him."

Thus the miles were gradually placed behind the singular couple, and the trail of which we have spoken was finally reached. Ooromoo turned and moved along that in the direction of the settlement, still keeping in the advance, alert, watchful, and never once allowing his vigilance to slacken.

Several more times he halted, and Aunt Cynthia, who continually watched him, guided herself by his signs, which she had learned to understand. What he observed at such times no one can say, for he prevented his companion from seeing it.

The sun had passed the meridian when Ooromoo again paused. The woman did the same, but he beckoned her to join him. She went forward unhesitatingly. He was smiling, but his extended hand, pointing in front, was not needed to make known a gratifying fact: they were close to the edge of the forest, and just beyond nestled the few cabins which made up the settlement of Warrenburg, while on the farther side towered the grim blockhouse known by the name of Fort Dinwiddie.

Aunt Cynthia's dangers were ended. She had

nothing more to fear from Nippinock cruelty or treachery.

She walked a few paces past her friend and guide, and as soon as she could control her emotions said:

"I understand now why you did this, Ooromoo; you knew when you spoke that bad word last night that it was wrong, and you deserved the cuff I gave you. This encourages me to persevere in the good way——"

At this point she turned her head to address the Nippinock more directly, but he had disappeared.

CHAPTER XXXVII

HOW SEVERAL THINGS HAPPENED

IT is now time to explain a number of occurrences with which the reader is familiar.

It has been made clear that Ooromoo was one of the most terrible warriors of the Nippinock tribe of Indians. He was the principal leader in the revolt, and insisted that his people should not wait, before taking the war-path, until the formal breaking out of the war between France and England.

Passing over a number of minor events, it will be recalled that when, by a daring piece of strategy, he secured admission into the Bothwell cabin, he received a ringing box upon the ear from Aunt Cynthia, because of an objectionable expression he uttered. Had he followed out his first impulse, he would have killed her on the spot, heedless of the two levelled rifles in the hands of Arthur Oakland and Stanton Bothwell; but the audacity of the act approached the sublime. Until then no living man would have dared to do such a thing. Yet the indignity had been put upon him by a defenceless woman, and she calmly confronted him without the first sign of fear of the consequences.

There is nothing in all the world that so appeals to a barbarous people as courage. By one of those strange workings of the heart, Ooromoo, in the twinkling of an eye, as may be said, was transformed from a ferocious enemy to a determined friend of Aunt Cynthia, though his feelings underwent no change as regarded the boys.

It has been said that when Ooromoo went from the cabin to meet Logan in deadly combat, he was resolutely determined to keep the engagement, but on his way thither he did some thinking. As he viewed the impending fight, he was absolutely certain to slay the Mingo, but by doing that he would deprive Aunt Cynthia of the only protector she had, for, environed as he was, he dare not let any of his people know of his change of sentiment toward one member of the hated race, and, forceful as was his personality, he was powerless in the face of so many fierce companions.

He therefore determined to postpone the meeting, though as resolute as ever that it should soon take place, for his enmity to the Mingo, whom he regarded as a traitor to his own people, was unquenchable. He avoided the rendezvous, but, reflecting that some understanding was necessary with him, he was about to go back, when, accidentally, they met, as has already been described.

Ooromoo, after a few exchanges of compliments,

made his remarkable proposal, which was that the two should unite to extricate the woman and boys (for he knew the parties could not be dissociated) from their situation, and, that being accomplished, they would then meet in their duel to the death.

It need not be said that the Mingo accepted the proposition, and it was he who outlined the clever scheme by which success was to be brought about. Ooromoo was to go several miles in the direction of the settlement, and then display the signal by which Great Bear, through some of his warriors, was to call the Nippinocks to leave the vicinity of the clearing and join the main party in its attack upon the settlement.

This strategy of course, could have been carried out by Logan, who learned the nature of the signal, but there were objections to his doing so, the most important of which was, that it would draw him away from his friends at a time when they were likely to need him. Moreover, there could be no objection whatever to Ooromoo's assuming the task.

The Mingo could not repress a certain suspicion that the Nippinock was playing him false, for it was unaccountable to Logan that an indignity done one of his race by a woman should change the warrior's hatred into regard; but Logan knew there could be no discounting the courage of Ooromoo, and no other pretext presented itself for his proposal to postpone the duel.

However, the Mingo climbed a tree which gave him the view he needed, and saw the signal as made by the Nippinock. The sight removed the last vestige of doubt, and, descending to the ground, Logan hurried to the clearing, meeting the smaller party on the way. This proved that the coast was clear and would remain so for several hours.

How Ooromoo should square matters with his comrades was his own problem. He probably explained that some frightened member of the war-party, lingering in the rear, had summoned them on his own responsibility, for a little farther on, when several of the scouts were encountered, it was learned that the alarm was a false one, and Ooromoo, apparently in a towering rage, hurried back with his companions to repair, if possible, the oversight.

The grace thus given our friends we know was well used, and they gained the opportunity which, but for the trick named, could never have been theirs.

It was more than two hours after the flight of the fugitives that Ooromoo and Leaping Deer made their reconnoissance, protected behind their odd shields, and it came to light that the whites were gone. The nest was warm, but the birds had flown.

Ooromoo now led his company eastward in a real effort to join Great Bear. When he did so, the party was on its return from the disastrous attack upon the settlement. The sullen and enraged Great Bear some time later ordered him with more than a dozen of their best scouts to shut off the flight of the fugitives to the blockhouse, and in his gnawing chagrin he threatened to put Ooromoo and every one of his party to death if they allowed even one of the whites to escape.

Among the numerous strange incidents connected with the events we have been relating were the following: Ooromoo and his comrades, on their return to the clearing, arrived about midway between the turn of night and daylight. Some hours later Great Bear and his warriors reached the spot and arrangements were completed for an unflinching pursuit and hunt of the fugitives. Captain Choteau's arrival was but a few minutes later than Great Bear's.

It was noon when James Oakland and Winslow Bothwell appeared at the old home of the latter and found the house empty. Cheered by the discovery, but still anxious, they turned back, hoping to be of assistance to the dear ones, who, they did not doubt, were making every possible effort to reach the settlement.

Thus it will be noted that several parties were travelling at the same time between the deserted cabin and Fort Dinwiddie. The brothers-in-law were hunting for those under charge of Logan, and though they must have passed near each other, the parties never suspected it, but the strangest fact of all was that Oakland and Bothwell made the entire journey back and returned without encountering a single Nippinock, though, as we know, the "woods were full of them." When this declaration was made some time later to the Mingo he bluntly said he did not believe it; nevertheless, it was true.

Captain Choteau also crossed the course of Oakland and Bothwell, but they did not meet, though the officer, without any thought on his part, ran into Logan's party and gave an impressive proof of the worth of his services before he had little more than time to make himself known.

The understanding between Ooromoo and Logan was that when the former, by drawing off his warriors who were besieging the cabin, opened the way for the escape of the whites, he performed his part of the contract. That much being done, everything now depended upon the Mingo, who looked for no further aid from his enemy, playing for the time the part of a friend.

When Logan discovered the moccasin imprints beside those made by the woman, he was certain of the worst. She had been captured by a Nippinock, who was conducting her to his comrades, with the intention of torturing her to death, in accordance with the hideous custom among most of the tribes of American Indians. Instantly all thought of the man and boys in his company vanished, and the Mingo broke into a run after the missing one.

He was handicapped by the necessity of keeping to the trail, for he could make no guesses as to the precise destination of the captor. In some places, where the ground was hard or stony, he was so delayed that he became desperate and actually lost the scent for a brief time. He never ceased his work, however, and by and by made a discovery which astonished him: Aunt Cynthia was under the escort of Ooromoo the Nippinock!

Logan continued hovering on the rear, not that he suspected Ooromoo's integrity, for all doubt was gone, but that he might give him help in any one of the numerous contingencies that were liable to arise. Fortunately, no occasion appeared for the services of the Mingo.

When the couple were within a quarter of a mile of the settlement Logan stopped following them. He was convinced that all danger had been passed, and it was the same as if Aunt Cynthia was within Fort Dinwiddie itself.

His next purpose was to press on at a moderate pace, so as to meet Ooromoo as he came back. The woman being taken care of and out of the way, what better opportunity could be asked for settling the affair between the two warriors?

One phase of the situation, however, caused the Mingo to play the part enacted by the Nippinock the night before. Captain Choteau and the boys were still several miles away, and the intervening space bristled with danger. The officer, because of his friendly relations with the Nippinocks, and despite the recent events, in which the part played behind him could not become known for some time, was in no special peril and doubtless would be able to take care of himself; but it was far otherwise as concerned Arthur and Stanton.

A consideration of the matter impressed the Mingo with the feeling that he had no right to let anything interfere with his duty to the youths, who, from this time forward, could expect not the slightest consideration from Ooromoo.

"When *they* have reached the settlement," was the thought of Logan, "nothing shall prevent the meeting between Ooromoo and me."

So it came about that the Mingo took the back trail until he met his three friends threading their course toward the settlement. With his assistance they safely wound their way through the labyrinth of dangers, and before the declining sun had reached the horizon, Captain Choteau, Arthur Oakland, and Stanton Bothwell were within the walls of Fort Dinwiddie, without one of the number having received so much as a scratch.

CHAPTER XXXVIII

CONCLUSION

AND so it came about that on the afternoon of the day following the siege of the cabin in the clearing all those who were thereby placed in imminent danger arrived at Fort Dinwiddie, none the worse because of the perils through which a watchful Providence had brought them.

Logan the Mingo parted with his friends on the edge of the wood and turned back into the wilderness. At last he was relieved of all responsibility. Ooromoo had more than fulfilled his part of the singular agreement, and was as ready to meet Logan as the latter was to meet him; but, knowing nothing of his immediate plans, the Nippinock made his way to his village, to confirm the report that not only had all the whites escaped, but the warriors who hunted them so persistently had suffered severely. Great Bear did not carry out his threat of punishing the survivors for their failure, for there would have been a savage protest against adding new victims to the fearful roll already made. Moreover, the main party under Great Bear himself had been the greatest sufferers.

Several weeks passed before Logan was able to get word to the Nippinock village that he was impatiently awaiting his antagonist. The reply that came back was a surprise. Ooromoo was no longer among the living. The particulars of his fate never became known, but the belief of the Mingo and of Captain Ned Hunter and his brother scouts was that in some way the Nippinocks learned the truth as to the false signal displayed by Ooromoo, and of his part in saving the fugitives, and that the vengeance which they visited upon him was natural and characteristic.

Captain Eugene Choteau was received with the utmost cordiality and friendship at the blockhouse, for no one could underestimate his services. Although he had declared to Great Bear that he purposed going to the fort to spy out its weakness, it need hardly be said he was not that sort of man. His country and England were still at peace, and "officially" remained so long after actual fighting began, and although the relations were severely strained, and although the Captain's business among the western Indians was well known, he was treated like the honored guest he was, and when, at the end of a few days, he took his departure it was with the regrets and best wishes of all.

Aunt Cynthia feelingly expressed her gratitude, and the gallant officer remarked confidentially to

Captain Hunter that he would he were worthy to ask her hand in marriage.

"Well, why the mischief don't you?" asked the blunt scout.

"Ah, zere is one leetle deeficulty in ze way, my good Captain."

"I can't see that there is,—what is it?"

"I hef one loafly wife in la belle France alretty. Ah, she is ze idol of my heart and I loaf her more zan my life!"

"Humph! that's different," grunted his friend.

Captain Choteau served all through the French and Indian War, was severely wounded at Quebec, but recovered and was promoted to the colonelcy which he had gallantly won.

The services rendered by Oakland and Bothwell were not important, but the fault was not theirs, since they were ready to go wherever needed; and it so happened that they were not called where severe fighting took place. Arthur and Stanton enlisted when the war was well under way, and both were wounded,—the former so severely that for a time his life hung in the balance; but, happily, he pulled through and both lived to take an active part in the War for Independence, and to enjoy the blessings which afterward came to their beloved country.

Perhaps reference should be made to one individual who was brought forward in the earlier pages of this work. He was a young Virginian named George Washington, who at that time was on his way with a letter from Governor Dinwiddie to the French commandant, five hundred miles distant in the West. He returned in due time to Williamsburg, the capital, and handed the reply to the governor. That reply, as you well know, meant WAR, which soon broke out between France and England and was prosecuted at first with the advantage on the side of the former, but in the end England triumphed and France was driven from the American continent.

In the French and Indian War, as well as in the Revolution that followed, and in the events down to the close of the eighteenth century, George Washington performed quite a creditable part, as perhaps you may have heard.

I am sure you wish to know something further about Logan the Mingo, and I am sorry to say it is a sad story. I have already told you that he was born about the year 1730 and was the son of Shikellamy, chief of the Cayugas; that his Indian name was Tah-gah-gute, and he received that of John Logan in memory of William Penn's secretary, James Logan, the devoted friend of the red men. He spent his early manhood on the frontiers of Pennsylvania and Virginia, and was held in high esteem by the whites because of his fine presence, his great courage, his integrity, and his many engaging qualities.

It was while he was living near Reedsville, Pennsylvania, with his family, that the Mingoes elected him their chief. About 1770, he removed to the banks of the Ohio, where, like Tecumseh, Red Jacket, and other prominent Indian leaders, he became addicted to drink. Four years later his family were massacred by settlers in revenge for the many outrages by the Indians. When Logan learned the truth, he sent a declaration of war to Colonel Michael Cresap, who, he believed, instigated the massacre, though such was not the fact. Logan began the war, and throughout a period of several months his warriors perpetrated frightful barbarities among the scattered settlers. It is said that Logan took thirty scalps with his own hand during the war, which was ended by an overwhelming defeat of the Indians at the mouth of the Great Kanawha.

Logan disdained to appear among the chiefs who afterward sued for peace. Lord Dunmore, Governor of Virginia, sent John Gibson as his messenger to invite the Mingo chieftain to the council. Logan led Gibson into the woods, told him the story of his wrongs, and sent back the following message, which has been printed and spoken thousands of times:

"I appeal to any white man to say if ever he entered Logan's cabin hungry and he gave him not meat; if ever he came cold and naked, and he clothed him not. [During the latter part of the last long and bloody war Logan withdrew to his cabin and urged his people to make peace.] Such was my love for the whites that my countrymen pointed as they passed and said, 'Logan is the friend of the white man.' I had even thought to have lived with you, but for the injuries of one man. Colonel Cresap, last spring, unprovoked, and in cold blood, murdered all the relatives of Logan, not even sparing my women and children.

"There runs not a drop of my blood in the veins of any living creature. This called on me for revenge. I have sought it; I have killed many; I have fully glutted my vengeance. For my country, I rejoice at the beams of peace. But do not harbor a thought that mine is the joy of fear; Logan never felt fear; he will not turn on his heel to save his life.

"Who is there to mourn for Logan? Not one."

The chieftain's habits of intemperance grew upon him, and he soon became only a wreck of the once magnificent warrior. In the summer of 1780, in one of his frenzied moments, he struck his second wife so violent a blow that he fled, believing he had killed her. While passing through the woods, between Detroit and Sandusky, he was overtaken by a party of Indians, who he supposed to be the avengers of his dead wife. Logan attacked them with such fierceness that one of his own nephews was forced to kill him in self-defence.

Regarding the pathetic speech of Logan, it so impressed Gibson, the messenger, that he repeated it to Lord Dunmore. It was taken down by an officer and printed in the *Virginia Gazette*, and has been preserved by Jefferson in his *Notes on Virginia*."

THE END.

Milton Keynes UK
Ingram Content Group UK Ltd.
UKHW040046180324
439604UK00006B/1042